George Wilson

Counsels of an Invalid

Letters on Religious Subjects

George Wilson

Counsels of an Invalid
Letters on Religious Subjects

ISBN/EAN: 9783744660884

Printed in Europe, USA, Canada, Australia, Japan

Cover: Foto ©Lupo / pixelio.de

More available books at **www.hansebooks.com**

COUNSELS OF AN INVALID

LETTERS ON RELIGIOUS SUBJECTS

By GEORGE WILSON M.D.

Late Regius Professor of Technology in the University of Edinburgh

MACMILLAN AND CO.

London and Cambridge

1862

TO

MY SISTER JEANIE

THESE LETTERS OF OUR BROTHER

GEORGE

ARE LOVINGLY INSCRIBED.

— —

'Jesus loved Martha and her sister, and Lazarus.

PREFACE.

THE Letters of George Wilson were among the most characteristic effusions of his genius. His intimate friends, with one consent, pronounced him the most delightful letter-writer of their circle; and it has been justly felt by the public, that of the great and varied merits of his biography, perhaps the chief is the skill and taste with which these memorials have been made to tell the tale of his life, and to paint the full picture of his character. After a selection of correspondence so copious and diversified, it may be thought by some that anything more is superfluous. This objection will disappear when it is known how small a proportion the published letters bear to the mass, not less interesting and attractive, which remains untouched. Probably many have hoped, with the writer of this Prefatory Note, that additional selections would be issued, and some, perhaps, have wished that, in such a case, these should be less miscellaneous and fragmentary than was demanded by the laws of biography, and should rather revolve around some one topic of central interest; while of all such topics, there can have been little difference of opinion that religion deserved the preference, both from its own paramount importance, and from the qualifications, in all respects high, in some singular, of the writer for treating it with success in the form of letters.

It must be gratifying to all in whose minds these wishes and expectations have, more or less, articulately taken shape, that they have been anticipated by the Editor of this deeply interesting volume. It is fortunate that various series of religious letters existed, addressed to correspondents of very different ages, necessities, and capacities, and embracing almost every variety of style, from that of a child's alphabet to the gravest theological discussion. The remarks on religious authors and church systems will please by their candour; and they are published without note or comment, as was due to a thinker so independent. One invariable feature of other letters of the writer, and even of many of his religious ones, hardly appears in this collection. The play of quaint and original humour is repressed, either by the trying circumstances of those to whom the letters are written, or by the supreme desire to teach and solemnize. The comparative absence of this lighter quality will be found to be amply compensated by the lucid statement and fresh illustration of Scripture truth, the vivid reflection of personal Christian experience, and the depth of sympathy alike with the sorrows of nature and the consolations of grace. It is believed that such statements as here abound, of the doctrines, precepts, and comforts of the gospel of Christ, in a style which combines the clearness and vigour of the best scientific writing with the artless ease of the familiar epistle, and which bears throughout the deep mark of faith perfected by suffering, must, through the Divine blessing, produce in a wide circle a large measure of the highest kind of good.

JOHN CAIRNS, D. D.

BERWICK-ON-TWEED.

ADDITIONAL NOTE.

To multiply words by way of introduction to
the letters which follow, is a needless task.
They who read them will not need to be told
that they are not given to the public to add to
the fame of the writer, but only more fully to
carry out the purpose with which they were
penned, namely, to help and comfort the lambs
of Christ's flock. Allusions to these letters in the
Memoir of my brother (pp. 364, 365) have caused
their publication to be ardently desired by many.
The haste with which some were written, in
time snatched from pressing business duties, has
left traces in the style; but this seems abundantly
compensated by the outgushing of Christian love
and tenderness manifested throughout, the prudence and wisdom of the counsels, and their
adaptation to the varied wants of God's children—

the young and those in mature years; the workers in life's busy scenes, and those laid aside in helplessness to suffer and to die. Many thanks are due to those who have permitted the publication of the letters in this little volume—their names are withheld by their own desire—and to Dr. Cairns for the foregoing pages.

JESSIE AITKEN WILSON.

ELM COTTAGE, EDINBURGH,
   May 1862.

COUNSELS OF AN INVALID.

LETTERS TO A YOUTH.

THE letters immediately following were written to a young friend whose studies were interrupted by severe and dangerous illness, apparently sapping the foundations of life. A gradual recovery happily removed anxiety, and, now settled in life, and actively engaged in its pursuits, he, with a grateful remembrance of the sympathy then shown, kindly permits the publication of the letters addressed to him.

January 7th, 1847.

DEAR D.,—I am afraid you must be thinking that I have totally forgotten you. I have not,

A

however ; but during the Christmas week, up even to Monday evening, I was so occupied with the congregational duty required at my hands, that I had not a disposable moment to write to you. Since Monday I have been so poorly, feverish, and unwell, that though I have twice sat down to write to you, I have had to give it up.

This morning I write a note to explain to you my silence. To-night, or to-morrow, or Sabbath, it will go hard with me but I shall write to you. Meanwhile, let me, in reference to one passage in your last letter, say that I do by no means look upon your state of health in the way you seem to think I do. Indeed, I never had the data from which to form even an approximative opinion as to the urgency of your malady. I only knew that you had been long ill, so long as to make yourself and your friends very anxious.

I am not disposed to think that your health is worse than mine : I hope it is a great deal better. My own hold on life, and prospect of length of years, are very feeble. Yours I have thought was somewhat less firm and distinct than could be wished also; and those who suffer like you and me, are not the victims of chronic maladies merely, whose effects we have to fear, but are made by our long illnesses far more liable than others are, to be attacked by sharp onsets of acute diseases. Without, therefore, attempting to weigh nicely in the balance the amount of your illness, I judged that you were ill.

But what, my dear friend, if you had threescore years and ten before you? Would that make God less desirable, or obedience to Him less a duty? The subjects we have been discussing together are not topics suited only to invalids, but as truly demanding the fullest consideration on the part of the robust, and as certainly fitted to make life joyful to the healthful, as no longer to let death be terrible to the unhealthy.

It would be best for all men that they were like you and me, parties whose lives no insurance office would have to do with, if at least the notion of their health is to make them hand over eternity to their sick brethren, as only concerning them.

Since we began to write to each other, hundreds of stronger men are gone to the other world: to many their health was a snare, and they were led by it to neglect all thought of a judgment to come. You and I would be guilty of tremendous folly, if we coaxed ourselves into the notion that we are not so very ill that we need to be 'ready' to die. We are in worse health than the stout people about us, and the stoutest may die to-morrow; how much more may we! Let that thought suffice us.

I would also say, Look not backwards. You speak of a season in early life when you had a faith in Christ such as you have not now. Well, we are all apt to think the past worse or better than it was, according to the mood we are in, in looking back on it. Perhaps you unwittingly conceive of that child-faith as clearer and deeper and fuller than it was. Suppose, however, you do not exaggerate it, nevertheless, be sure that the faith which was sufficient for the child would not content the man. You have difficulties which you had not then; doubts and perplexities which at an earlier age did not disturb you. If your child-faith in all its fulness were given back to you, you would be the first to be startled by its meagreness. It would not carry you above your *present* sorrows and anxieties. My dear friend, faith, hope, and love, the three great Christian virtues, of their nature tend to become infinite. However great the amount of them any Christian possesses, he might possess incalculably more. God can grant you a far fuller faith than your child-faith, however full it was. The great apostolic maxim is, '*Forgetting* the things that are behind,' the amount of attainment already made. Read the passage for yourself (Phil. iii. 13), and see what Paul thought of his earlier faith ; it was good but not *best*. There was something *better* before him : therefore he 'pressed on.' Press you on too, dear friend ; God will feed you with the meat which you must now eat, instead of the babes' milk you sucked before. He will give you a man's faith. In great haste, your affectionate,

GEORGE WILSON.

January 15*th*, 1847.

DEAR D.,—I thank you very cordially for your
kindness in getting the crystals, and will accept
them (as a passionate crystal-lover) for their own
sakes, and secondly, and especially, as loving you
for your sake.

Since you desire to read the *Vestiges*, I send
you the loan of a copy, in returning which you
need be in no hurry. As for other books, if you
have not read Humboldt's *Kosmos*, I strongly recommend it ; also, the Bridgewater Treatises,
especially Dr. Whewell's, and Drs. Roget and
Buckland, as well as Sir Charles Bell's. You
would be pleased, I think, with Whewell's *History of the Inductive Sciences*, and Philosophy
of the Same. Sir John Herschel's Treatises on
Optics, and on Astronomy and Natural Philosophy (the latter two are accessible in the Ca-
binet Library), are also very pleasant and instructive volumes.

In the way of literature, I suppose you confine
yourself to prose. If you can lay hands on a

volume by Isaac Taylor, called *Saturday Evening*, I think you would greatly relish it. The *Essays* by John Foster, I can also strongly recommend, and I will think of other works for you.

I have not abandoned the thought of trying the hydrogen experiment, but for the last fortnight I have been unable to work in the laboratory, and have had to spend as much time as I could lying on the sofa. . . .

You asked me, in a former letter, to refer you to some of those delights of heaven which might suffice to lessen that hold of the world which, as we all find, keeps us from realizing God's command to ' set our affections on things above.'

The great difference between heaven and earth consists in there being no sin in the former ; and the replacement of sin by holiness is the cause, directly or indirectly, of all the joy that prevails in the abode of the blessed. Our sufferings, physical and moral, have all flowed, mediately or immediately, from our own sins, or those of others, up to Adam, in whose transgression we all fell. Sin and suffering are inseparable ; and if

in this life we find the one, the other, we may
be sure, is not far off. Holiness and happiness
are equally inseparable, and wherever the first
abounds in this world, the last will be found in
large measure. In this life, however, a multitude
of causes prevent holiness securing the amount of
happiness it is able to produce. To mention but
one, the tortures of physical agony, the pangs of
hunger, and the fatigue which daily necessary
labour occasion, limit, and must lessen the happiness of the happiest. The holiest of men,
moreover, is an offender in many things ; sins,
and suffers because he sins ; and has a sensitiveness to the transgression of God's law, which
makes the slightest infraction of it the source of
a misery to him which less holy men do not suffer from the commission of greater sins. This is
never to be forgotten ; but after due allowance
has been made for it, it remains to be noticed,
that no man is happy in this world to the extent
that he is holy, whereas in heaven he would be,
and the holiness there being complete, the happiness is also.

We think, in this life, of happiness as one thing, and holiness as another, and hunger a great deal more after the former than the latter; but in heaven they think only of the holiness as the thing to be realized, and the happiness is found to be inseparable from it. It comes without special search for it, being a necessary concomitant of the sinlessness. If we would only leave happiness to look after itself, and be content to struggle after holiness, we should without effort come into the possession of what we so vainly and sinfully seek to procure. Surely, then, we need no other reason for longing for heaven than this one, that it is a place where sin does not, and cannot enter. Everything conceivable of delight is involved and implied in the one thing—NO SIN.

Of the *positive* joys of heaven we can form no conception; but its negative delights form a sufficiently attractive picture,—no pain; no thirst; no hunger: no horror at the past; no fear of the future: no failure of mental capacity; no intellectual deficiency: no morbid imaginations; no follies; no stupidities: but above all, no insulted feelings; no wounded affections; no despised love or unrequited regard : no hate, envy, jealousy or indignation of or at others : no falsehood, dishonesty, dissimulation, hypocrisy, grief or remorse. In a word, to end where I began, no sin and no suffering.

Think what we should be, in this world even, if we had painless, healthy bodies, clear, undimmed intellects, and moral faculties never disturbed, misdirected, thwarted or outraged. We shall have all these in heaven, and infinitely more. Glorified bodies, expanded intellects, and holy hearts shall be ours. God shall be the teacher, the subject the infinite ; the scene the universe ; and the time eternity. We must be poor fools indeed, if we do not think, that after the soberest calculation of the relative joys of this world and the next, it would not be far better to be with Christ, than here.

February 10*th*, 1847.

DEAR D.,—I am very sorry that you are not to be with me soon, and willingly write, since that is the case. In truth, I would have written, when

I saw from B.'s letter that you were poorly, had it not been that I was unwell myself. I have been overworked since Christmas, and when I did at last get a rest, a reaction of disordered health came, out of which I have not yet emerged. Pain unfits one much less for thought, as you know, than sickness, headache, and a disordered body. I have accordingly excused myself from writing any but business letters.

Meanwhile, I address you a mere line from the Laboratory, to assure you of sympathy. I take shame and blame to myself, for not having told you how much I valued the specimens you sent. Those remarkable drusy cavities in the trap-rock are most curious things, and well worth keeping.

As to Reviews, the *Edinburgh*, *Quarterly*, and *North British*, have always some articles well worth reading. I read them all, and relish them all. The British Quarterly, I suppose you cannot get at ; if you can, it is readable also. I like the *Edinburgh* best. I do not recommend the *Westminster :* it is in bad hands, and has a most unpleasant religious, often quite infidel tone.

You need not have returned the *Vestiges* till you were done with it. It is a pleasantly written book. The author is master of a fine rhetorical style, but he is a poor, very poor logician, and blunders often most foolishly. I scarcely, indeed, know a writer on science who has a more vague way of referring to matters which ought to have been sharply and precisely defined.

In vain have I endeavoured over and over again to discover what is his exact theory of animal development, but either the author fancies he has made things very clear where he has not, or he purposely mystifies. I am much inclined to think that he is partly an unintentional, partly a willing deceiver. Any way, a great deal of the book is stolen from others, and it is full of blunders, which only the complacent, easy-going style of the writer prevents from being detected by casual readers. I hold the author and his philosophy very lightly.

Can you suggest to me any religious topic on which you think I could at all serve or interest you by writing? Are there not some points on which you feel that your knowledge might be in-

creased? Some relations of God, which might be
made clearer? I think you are quite right to decline unbosoming yourself as to your religious state.
I am altogether opposed to the practice of *confession* to another mortal as a general practice. I
neither expect, therefore, nor wish that you should
reveal your feelings, unless you think that some
service could be done you as a result of this. But
there are many things you must think and doubt
about, on which you could write without invading
or exposing the sanctuary of your own sacred
thoughts. The end, our great end, of our faith,
the Apostle tells us, is the 'salvation of our souls.'
Peace and joy are spoken of as necessary results
of believing. There is a perfect love described
which casteth out fear. Now, my dear friend, if
we have not some considerable share of peace,
and joy, and love, notwithstanding bodily illness
or other outward distress, there is something
wrong or wanting in our knowledge of and relation to God.

I am here suddenly required to stop, but I will
write to you soon ; and if there be any religious, as

well as literary or scientific matter on which you think I could help you, please say so, and I'll write.

.

November 9th, 1847.

I WAS not a little surprised at your chemical speculation, as I have long entertained the same view, and, oddly enough, was thinking over it again yesterday, to settle the best way of testing it by experiment.

A galvanic circle cannot be formed without a liquid between the pairs, so that I am afraid the combination of hydrogen and oxygen, as gases round platina, could not be considered a phenomenon of the same kind as the combination of oxygen with zinc in a galvanic battery. In this instrument, decomposition is as essential to the evolution of electricity, as combination. It is not enough, for example, that the zinc plate of a battery should combine with oxygen. The O[1] must not be free, but must be liberated from a state of combination (as from HO) the moment it com-

---

[1] O is the symbol for Oxygen : H for Hydrogen.

bines with Zn,[1] otherwise there is no electricity. Another objection to the phenomenon you refer to being looked upon as galvanic, is the fact that glass and sand cause H and O to unite at a temperature much below that necessary for their ignition, when these bodies are not present. It is quite true that the glass must be heated before it produces this effect, but not highly; and after all, it is only a difference in degree, not one in kind between glass or sand and platina. The one makes hydrogen and oxygen unite at 60°, the other at 300°, or thereabout.

These are mere minor matters, however. Your fundamental conception of hydrogen, if a metal, being able to form one of a galvanic pair, I cordially assent to. I think there is no likelihood of the electricity produced by a single pair, of which hydrogen was one, having intensity enough to affect a gold-leaf electroscope. Magnetic or chemical effects are more hopeful. Now comes the question, How are we to arrange hydrogen and our *other* metal so as to have a pair? I got

[1] Zn, the symbol for Zinc.

my notion how it is to be done from Grove. You are not, probably, acquainted with his gas battery. I strongly incline to think that it contains the demonstration of the truth of *our* view. It is a very curious instrument, whatever be the explanation of it. It consists essentially of a series of test tubes, standing with their mouths down in acidulated water. The first, to the left, is partially filled with hydrogen, the second with oxygen, the third with H, the fourth with O, and so on for any number of tubes you please. In each tube is a plate of platina, which ends in a platina wire, passing hermetically through the shut end of the tube. When the battery is arranged, the wire from an oxygen tube in one vessel of acid water is joined to the wire in the H tube in the *next* vessel; and at one end there is an incomplete O wire, and at the other a free H wire, as in a metal battery, there is a free zinc at one end, and a free copper at the other. This singular instrument has all the powers of ordinary batteries. It decomposes water, gives sharp shocks and sparks, and whirls about magnetic needles. The gases disappear in the tubes as the instrument is in action, and from time to time must be replenished. There is here, you will observe, an essential difference from the mere union of H and O in a tube by platina.

The H combines not with free O, but with the O of the water in the same tube, disengaging H. The O combines in the next tube, with the H of water in it, disengaging O. The puzzle is to say how the platina acts. If it merely metallically connects the H and O, then *our* case is as good as proved; but if, as I much fear, it acts specifically, our view is doubtful.

I propose the following arrangement. In the first place, I published in 1839 the proof that H, as a metal, excels all the noble metals in positive characters. I would avoid platina and take gold, as I know certainly that it would act to hydrogen in a pair (galvanic) as zinc does to copper. The liquid must be some component of hydrogen: H O is too powerful; so is Hcl.[1] I propose hydriodic acid. I would take, like Grove, two tubes, put a

---

[1] Hydrochloric acid.

plate of gold in each, and bring them through a wire, as he does. I would fill the one tube with the aqueous solution of H I,[1] and the other partially with H. I would not have a gas in each tube, like Grove, but a gas in one, and a liquid in another; and I would not let the gold dip into the liquid in the H tube. I intend the gold there simply to act as a metal,—a continuation, as it were, of the H. My hope is that the gold in the liquid would have hydrogen liberated at it, and that the H in the other tube would combine with iodine, and form hydriodic acid. If it succeeded, the action of the metals in the tubes would alternate.

I fell upon this plan last spring, when lecturing in the Music Hall on Electricity, and talked of trying it; but I was too poor for the gold, and too distrustful of my manipulative dexterity, to feel courage enough to venture on an experiment of much delicacy. I have just been lecturing on Hydrogen, when back came the sleeping idea. I was thinking over it yesterday, and fairly jumped when I opened your letter to-day. I have not

[1] Hydriodic acid.

rested till we exchanged ideas on this curious matter.   Do you think my experiment promising, or
can you suggest a better, and I'll have it tried?
Should I ever publish on the matter, you shall
have honourable mention as having held the gal-
vanic-hydrogen thought. . . . .

This is an extra hydrogenous letter.   On the
far more important contents of your letter which
I have not noticed, I shall write on Sabbath.   It
is a great length to know that we ought to submit
to God.   The good Spirit who has taught you this
will, I pray God, carry you further.

Your attached friend.

November 26th, 1847.

DEAR FRIEND,—Nothing, I am sure, will give
me more pleasure than to correspond with you, if
that will, in any degree, interest or amuse you in
your present illness.   If you are to be amused,
interested, or edified, moreover, we must select
other topics than my papers, which will not set
the world on fire.

My dear D., had it pleased God to grant us

bodily health, I venture to say that we should both have done something to help forward the great cause of science, and have earned the love and respect of our fellow-men. But it is plain, from the wasting illnesses God has sent us, that he does not need us as expositors of the laws he, the great Chemist, has imposed upon his own universe; neither you nor I, in all human probability, will be long left to study earthly chemistry. We shall very soon, I anticipate, be called away from seeing all things through a glass darkly, to meeting God face to face, and shall have to answer to him for the deeds done in the body. We should certainly exhibit the most inordinate vanity if we thought that the great mass of our fellow-men would be losers by our being swept off the great chess-board of a world. This board, indeed, is always so crowded that, with the exception of our attached relations and a few friends, the greater number of our neighbours will be glad to know that our being cleared away has left more elbow-room. Think how soon the world gets over the death of a

Chalmers or an O'Connell, and let us be content that the place that knew us once shall know us no more.

I am persuaded, from what I have experienced, that the world fills but a small space in the thoughts of one near to death. I believe, from what I have felt when brought very near to the grave, that the engrossing, devouring idea is that of one's own individuality or personality, and of God's personality. The prevailing feeling is that of the great Judge waiting for our soul, as if there were no other soul in existence, and we, in our naked spirituality, without one relative, earthly friend, or well-wisher, about to pass away into the darkness and stand before God. You and I, D., had need to be thinking of this. No transmutation which chemist or alchymist ever hoped for, or ever realized, has equalled or can equal the strangeness of that transformation which we shall undergo when we gasp out of this life into the next. Chemistry will not help us there, nor to have read or written papers. ' If there be knowledge, it shall vanish away.' If I do not

give you pain or offence by writing thus, I will
write to you soon again; but I shall wait to hear
from you.

Monday Evening.

I add a note craving you to excuse the desul-
toriness of the remarks I send. I shall write
(with your permission) as soon again as possible.
With nine lectures a week, and laboratory and
other work, I can only snatch an interval now
and then for writing.

I should feel much pleased if you would commit to paper the chemical speculations which
you spoke of. It would be interesting to yourself, and very much so to me. Our ideas may
be realized by others, if not by ourselves. God
gave David credit for designing to build Him a
temple, although he did not build it; and we
may enjoy the satisfaction of revealing a new
idea, though it may not fall to our lot to work
it out into a certain truth. . . . . . .

May 'the God of all consolation' comfort and
direct you, lead you out of darkness into light,
and give you joy and peace in believing!

December 5th, 1847.

DEAR D.,—I write to you in the quiet stillness of a Sabbath night, and will, therefore, leave till to-morrow any reference to secular things. We shall have a grave conversation together concerning the worthiest objects that can occupy men's thoughts, and we shall begin by imploring that God's Holy Spirit, who has been promised to all who ask for Him, may guide us into that truth, which without His aid we cannot attain.

In a single letter it will be impossible to do more than take up some single topic, nor will it be possible to exhaust that; neither am I about to deliver anything like orderly, methodical pre-lections: quite otherwise, I intend only to speak on paper what could much better be talked over between us, were we together.

The great object all men aim after is happiness. They differ greatly as to what happiness is, and how it is to be attained; but there exists no sane being who does not, secretly or avowedly, consciously or unconsciously struggle after it; nor

is there any amount of it such, in largeness, that
the over-delighted man will cry, 'Hold! enough!'
Selfishness is no necessary element of this thirst-
ing after happiness, though it degrades and de-
bases all the seeking after happiness that is found
in this earth.   It is otherwise in heaven; the
spirits of just men made perfect, and the unfallen
angels, doubtless find it one, indeed, *the one* element of their unbroken, unalloyed happiness, that
though each is happy to the full, no amount of
selfishness mixes in his happiness.   He himself
is happy, not at the expense of the happiness of
others, but in proportion to the intensity and the
amount of the joy of others.   Only those sons of
Adam who have learned to abolish love of self
as the supreme passion, and have been taught of
God to love him with all their soul and strength
and might, and to love their neighbours as themselves, have achieved true happiness.

In the last sentence, I have anticipated; but
the object of what I have written is to express
this belief, viz., that no one ought, as I think
many thoughtful young men like you are apt to do,

to be afraid to acknowledge, that to be as happy as possible (for to be as happy as we wish to be we soon find an unrealizable object in this world), is the chief aim of all our thoughts and actions. This premised ; we have next to ask, how are we to procure this desirable happiness? It seems to me that in striving to grasp this 'one thing needful,' the first thing that we have to realize is, that we are not self-existent, self-sustaining, independent beings ; but, on the other hand, enjoy only a conditional existence, and are sustained by another on whom we are completely dependent. In other words, we are creatures.

You will be disposed, my dear friend, to imagine that I am determined to begin with the very alphabet of knowledge, when I gravely tell you, as if you did not know and believe it, that you are a creature. I will tell you in reply, what was the case with myself. I was long out of my teens before I realized that I was a creature. I did not think that I had created myself; I did not doubt that God had made me. I had great fear and much reverence for God, and some love for him.   I would have been very glad to have exchanged the fear for perfect love, but that did not seem at the time attainable, and I did not make it my great object to reach it.   On the other hand (though I would not have confessed that to any one, and did not perceive, as I now do, the fact myself), I *practically* held by the doctrine that God had one circle of occupation, and I another, which, though immeasurably smaller than his, was nevertheless *mine.*   I should have been very glad to have been sure that this little supposed private or independent property was really and absolutely mine by a valid and unimpeachable title-deed.   In the secret recesses of my nature, I greatly doubted the validity of my claim, and conscience whispered that it was God's property, not mine.   But I would never confess to this belief, and struggled against acknowledging it.   I had no doubt that God had the *power* to dispossess me of my fancied possession, but I did my best to persuade myself that he had no *right*. I was willing to acknowledge Him as my superior, as a great baron vows fealty to his emperor, and I desired to have his favour, and to avoid his wrath ; but, like a turbulent lord, I was bent upon maintaining *my* rights, as well, nay far more than God's. I have prayed the God and Father of our Lord Jesus Christ, to forgive me these blasphemous thoughts, and I have found, with the psalmist, that there is forgiveness with God that he may be feared.

I shall leave it with your conscience to decide whether you have such feelings as I have confessed to ; and next week we shall consider how our guilt is deepened by our not being perfect creatures, like the good angels, but beings who lost in Adam the perfection of our nature.

Monday.

I intended, as you will perceive from the concluding lines of the preceding sheet, to have sent it alone, but I have thought it better, as the argument was incomplete, to continue to-day.

It will not be disputed, I think, by any one, that whatever an Almighty Being, who has no

equal or superior, creates, must be entirely dependent on that Creator for everything it possesses. If the Creator were not almighty, and the
highest existence, some higher and mightier being
might take the lesser Creator's work out of his
hand, and make it dependent on the superior.
But if we believe that we are creatures of the
Almighty, we must acknowledge that we *must* be
what he is pleased to make us, and can appeal
to no one else to pluck us out of his hand, if
we are dissatisfied with the gifts God has given
us. We are not, then, self-sustaining existences,
who can lay down laws for ourselves ; but have
no other choice than to accept the laws God has imposed on us, whether we approve of them or not.
This, I think, is the first canon in the search for
happiness ; yet practically it is every day neglected
by thousands. They are content if they can
gratify their own wills, and forget to inquire whether their Creator has sanctioned such gratifica-
tion. God's laws cannot be broken with impunity;
a punishment follows the breach of any one, and
so happiness is missed.

Seeing then that we are altogether at the mercy of God, and must obey his laws, or pay the exacted penalty for breaking them, our second question, as we would be happy men, will be, 'Are God's laws of such a kind that perfect obedience to them is likely to conduce to our joy, or should we rather dispute them as far as we can?' We could suppose an evil being like Satan creating conscious existences, and imposing laws on them, obedience to which entailed only the greatest misery, so that if possible, it would be the manifest interest of such creatures to disobey their creator.

Our Creator is no such being; 'His tender mercies are over all his works.' He is not only the Almighty, but the All-just, the All-good, the All-merciful, the All-holy—all his attributes are infinite. When He created Adam, he did not say to him, 'I created you and am Almighty; are you willing to submit your will to mine?' He showed our first parent that his happiness was one great object of his creation. He dignified Adam by forming him in his own image; he conferred upon him noble bodily and mental gifts ; he surrounded him with all that could contribute to his felicity, and permitted him, like a beloved child, to hold constant communion with his Almighty parent. God, as it were, said to Adam, ' I have satisfied you that I love you, and have your interest at heart : I have shown you that the laws I lay upon you are such as will secure the greatest perfection and joy of which your nature is susceptible. Are you willing, for I have left you a choice, to submit your will to mine in all things, and to trust to me as one that will never wrong you ? Choose ! I am the Sovereign ; you are the subject. My glory I will not give to another. In perfect obedience you will find perfect happiness : in disobedience, utter woe.' Adam fell. He forgot that he was a creature. Satan persuaded him that it was possible for him, instead of learning what was good and what was evil from God, to become a law unto himself on these matters, and so to become an independent existence beyond the reach of God's laws and power.

Every son of Adam has imitated his parents' guilt. None of us were, like him, created innocent, and therefore we could not, like him, fall. But we have all, who have come to reasonable years, deliberately disowned our creatureship, done our best to be independent of God, and been content to gratify our own wishes, without asking whether they were God's wishes or not. Is it a wonder we are all so unhappy? God permits us to disobey His laws, but does not allow us to escape the punishment of disobedience. And if in one sense we are more excusable than Adam was, inasmuch as we are less perfect; in another we are less so. For if the perfect man, with faculties entire, was guilty of the greatest folly in disowning his dependence, and pretending to be able to sustain himself, how much more foolish are we, whose imperfection has increased our dependence, in seeking to maintain that we are monarchs, and not subjects of the Great King!

Now, my dear friend, can you get the length of acknowledging that you are a creature, a subject, a dependant. If you can — and it is surely im-

possible to avoid acknowledging that you are ----
we come next to the momentous question, What
are God's laws that must be kept? Is it in man's
power to obey those laws fully? If it be not, as
it certainly is not, is there any way in which
man's happiness can be secured, although he
yields only an imperfect obedience?

Your affectionate friend.

Sabbath.

DEAR FRIEND,—A local complaint, which lames
me, shuts me in from church, and I spend a portion of the day, in consequence, in writing to
you.   We have agreed to acknowledge ourselves
dependent creatures, and confessed God's right
and power to require our obedience to his laws,
especially because ' these commandments are not
grievous.'   But here arises the great difficulty,
which you yourself have stated, namely, that no
conviction of the recompense that will attend
obedience is sufficient to induce us to obey. We
are perfectly persuaded that a particular act or

line of conduct will in the end only involve us in misery, and yet we deliberately do it. We can eloquently urge upon others, or upon ourselves, the madness of what we are about to do. Conscience foretells the remorse and agony we shall feel, and shows the certain punishment close at hand. But all this does not stop us. We are, as sinners, morally insane. Our wills are palsied, and we wish we were good men, but are at much pains to act as wicked ones.

At some period or other of their lives, most religiously educated persons have made a strong effort to keep God's laws. But the result, even when most satisfactory, has always been that the attempt has proved an utter failure, and the hopelessness of maintaining a perfect obedience has been realized most by those who have gone farthest beyond their fellows in obeying. Here, then, is a great dilemma. God will have a perfect obedience, or none at all. He that offendeth in one thing, offendeth in all. Not one jot or tittle will be excused us if we undertake to obey the laws. We may not pick and choose among the divine commandments. God's laws are all just and holy; to forgive breach of one because another had been obeyed, would be stamping the broken law as less just and imperative than the law which had been kept. An all-holy, wise, and just Lawgiver cannot cast discredit on his laws. The whole universe is looking to Him to maintain its rules, and would be perilled by the unforgiven, or unatoned-for, or unpunished breach of one. But further, man cannot keep *one* of God's laws, much less all of them. We are not debtors to God, who can engage to pay him very nearly all that he demands, and then beseech him to forgive us the trifling remainder that is over. We owe him millions, and have not so much as grains of dust to offer him by way of composition.

God, then, on the one hand, stands before us, requiring a perfect obedience to his law; and man stands on the other, unable to obey. If there be no other parties in the universe but God, in his awful character of an unrelenting Lawgiver, and fallen man, a wretched sinner, never able to satisfy his own sense of justice, but condemned by his own conscience before God's condemnation reaches him, there can be but one issue, — the Lawgiver will become the avenger, and the disobedient sinner suffer the punishment of his contempt of God's law.

Is there any direction in which we can look for help? Can any of the angels, 'that excel in strength,' engage to be surety for us,—promise to obey the law for us,—thus honour and justify it, and leave God, without a stain on his government, to forgive us, on account of the double obedience? Alas! the excellent strength of the angels failed many of them who fell, and goes no further than to enable each to render the homage due to God from him, and leaves no surplus to be bestowed on man. Moreover, the strength is all of God's giving and sustaining, for the angels are creatures as well as we. But this is the least of the difficulty : our surety, if we can find one, must not only obey for us, but suffer for us. The penalty must be exacted, the debt paid, and the justice of God's law witnessed to by the punishment of the transgressor or his substitute. And then it is not the sins of one man, but of all men, that are to be suffered for, and propitiation made for the sins of the whole world. There is no created being who could bear the wrath of God poured out upon the representative of the guilt of a world. He could not endure the tremendous punishment, nor offer a perfect obedience. Unless God himself help us, then, we are beyond remedy.

We might be tempted to think He could assist us thus : Seeing that every man has broken his laws, might not God make them less stringent, and not be so exacting in his demands? There is terrible impiety in such a thought. He who seriously entertains it, plainly affirms that God is an imperfect and unjust being. A human lawgiver may make unwise laws, and show his wisdom by softening or repealing them; but God's laws are the expression of perfect wisdom and justice. They cannot be bettered, and cannot be lowered in their claims, and annulled because too severe. The law (the moral law) is holy, just, and good, and must be 'magnified' and made honourable.

God himself has devised the remedy. He has

found out the means of remaining just, and, at the same time, of justifying sinners on certain terms. You know that the Bible teaches that God manifests himself as the Father, the Son or Word, and the Spirit. The Trinity is a profound mystery to us; but if the Bible be true, its existence is certain, and, when considering religion practically, we need not distract ourselves with metaphysical questions as to its nature. What it concerns us to believe is, that a distinct personality belongs to the Father, Son, and Spirit; and that nevertheless (however inconceivable to human intellect the idea is), they are one. The unity of the Trinity is, I think, a very practical question, and therefore I urge it. It is because Christ was God, that he was *able* to suffer even the infliction of the Father's wrath. It is because he was God, that he was *willing* to endure to the uttermost the punishment which otherwise would have fallen on the guilty. It is because he was God, that he could render a quite perfect obedience; and it was for the same reason that he had the infinite love that made him 'freely give himself to the death for us all.' It is essential, I

think, to our faith in the Bible, and in Christ, that
we should be satisfied of the sufficiency of our
surety ; that we should be certain that he has not
undertaken more than he can fulfil.   Now the New
Testament tells us that Christ 'thought it not robbery to be equal with God,' and that 'the Word
was God.'   If, then, we believe this, we cannot
but rest assured of this, that if we can obtain
Christ as our surety, we shall possess in him, at
least, an all-sufficient Advocate with the Father.

The New Testament further makes known to us
that Christ was born of a woman, and made under
the law.   'The Word was made flesh, and dwelt
among us.'   Here, again, is a great mystery ; but
let us remember we are warned that 'great is the
mystery of godliness ;' look only at its practical
bearing.   Christ was at the same time God and
man.   I have dwelt on the importance of believing in our Saviour's divinity, but it is not the less
important to believe in his humanity.   He could
not have been an example to us had he not been
man.   He is the 'first-born of many brethren ;'
'our elder brother.'   He could not have suffered

for man, but as man; and for many, many other
reasons, the certainty 'that he was tried and
tempted in all points like as we are,' is a most
precious and essential part of the doctrine of the
New Testament. One thing, however, is above
all insisted on, viz., that Christ was a sinless man.
He was 'without sin;' 'holy, harmless, undefiled,
and separate from sinners.'

I could wish to write a great deal more, but I
am fairly fatigued. I shall, therefore, reserve for
the next letter the continuation. In the meanwhile, my dear friend, pray to God for forgiveness,
help, and light. I will pray for you, but neglect
it not yourself. 'Come unto me, all ye that labour,
and are heavy laden, and I will give you rest.' That
includes you. I found it included me in my darkest
days. 'If any man lack wisdom, let him ask of
God, that giveth liberally, and upbraideth not.'
Take God at his word. Put only as much faith
in his statements as you do in those of your kind,
earthly father, and you will find that he is more
willing to give than you to receive. Say only, with
the publican, 'God be merciful to me a sinner!'

·The Lord bless you, and keep you and yours from all evil !

December 16th, 1847.

DEAR FRIEND,—I had set the whole of this evening aside, intending to write to you, but I have been unusually interrupted, and can only write a few, a very few, lines.

I can profoundly sympathize with your feelings of agitation, agony, and alarm, at finding your strength and health failing, and another world looking closer at hand than it did a short time ago. I have been in this condition, and only passed out of it after a spiritual struggle such as I still feel appalled in gazing back upon. In reference to your question, whether God gradually reveals himself, I will at once answer, that no man ever became a perfect Christian at once, or even reached to be that during a whole lifetime. St. Paul, the inspired apostle, one of the holiest of men, did not think that he had attained to perfection, or was already perfect.

Nevertheless, it is not the less true that the least advanced Christian is separated by a distinct line of demarcation from the unconverted man. The one is blind, the other sees, not with perfect, full, and unbroken vision, but he sees enough to make him safe for time and eternity, and will every day see more and more clearly. The other does not see at all.

You, my dear friend, however, are looking in the wrong direction for peace and joy. These are not to be found by looking into our hearts to discover if faith, and hatred of the world and of Satan, are there. 'The heart is deceitful above all things, and desperately wicked,' says one inspired writer. Another adds, 'If we say that we have no sin, we deceive ourselves, and the truth is not in us ;' and continues, 'If we confess our sins, he (namely, God) is faithful and just to forgive us our sins, and to cleanse us from all unrighteousness.' 'The blood of Jesus Christ his Son cleanseth us from all sin.'

Look away from yourself altogether, and fix your eyes solely on the 'Lamb of God, which taketh away the sin of the world.' Do you believe that Christ died for all who will accept him as their surety? If you do not (and you feel that to be the case), get the Testament, and read and pray over it. This is the way, the only way. I would suggest a thoughtful, prayerful reading, at suitable intervals, but as much as possible, of St. John's Gospel and Epistles, and of the Epistles to the Hebrews, the Ephesians, and the Romans. Read and study earnestly what is said of Christ and the great scheme of salvation, and forget not that the conditions laid down by an apostle are simply these, ' Believe on the Lord Jesus Christ, and thou shalt be saved.' If you cannot believe on him, still read the Bible and pray, and read the Bible and pray, and again, and again; but however dark or desponding your feelings may be, dwell not on them; fly from them to Christ.

God, my friend, has not forgotten or overlooked you. It is His good Spirit that has given you the sense of sin you have. Thank him for that: offer up your thanksgivings, that he has given you some sense of your need of a Saviour. Ask him to increase this sense, and to grant you the Saviour you need ; but avoid analysis of your own feelings ; look out of yourself up to God, and at Christ bleeding for you on the Cross.   Here is a text worth much : ' God was in Christ, reconciling the world unto himself, not imputing their trespasses unto them.'

The post-hour is close at hand : I'll write again to-morrow more carefully.

.

December 17*th*, 1847.

MY DEAR FRIEND,—I again sit down to write to you a few lines.   You must not think me unkind or indifferent if I write hurriedly, for I lectured for nearly three hours to-day, and spent two with my pupils in the laboratory.   I feel, in consequence, scarcely able to do justice to the great and momentous matter about which you and I are so much and so justly concerned.

I would begin by observing that I have often been struck by that remarkable text, ' He that cometh to God must believe that he is, and that he

is a rewarder of those that diligently seek him.'
Do you pray because you think it a duty, or do
you pray *expecting* an answer? There are many
Christians who will confess that for years of their
lives before their conversion, they prayed only
from a sense of duty, and really, in their secret
hearts, never looked for a reply. This, my dear
friend, is mocking God. He has said, 'Ask and
it shall be given you; seek, and ye shall find;
knock, and it shall be opened unto you.' The
great majority of even those who have Bibles to
read, and have heard of Christ, do not really look
upon those statements as honest affirmations.
They do not take God at his word. They pray
to be forgiven, but they have often no desire to be
forgiven (which is not assuredly your case), and
what is as bad, and may perhaps apply to you,
they do not expect to be forgiven, as a child believes that a loving father who has promised to
forgive an offence, if forgiveness be asked, goes
with confidence to his parent, and asks, expects,
and obtains pardon.

Now, do you really believe that God hears and

answers prayer? It is a great matter to be quite certain that he does. The Bible assures us not only that God will *permit* us to ask favours of him, will *submit*, as it were, to turn from governing the universe to listen to us; but, on the other hand, the Scriptures assure us that God willingly listens, delightedly hearkens to the petitions of his creatures. Nay, what is more, we are assured that God will not blame us for importunity. We are, like Jacob, to wrestle with God, and not to give up till we receive a blessing. Think of that remarkable parable told in the beginning of the 18th chapter of St. Luke's Gospel, of the widow and the unjust judge, which the Saviour himself spoke to teach that 'men ought always to pray and not to faint.' Here unceasing importunity is commanded, the ground for listening to her request being, 'her continual coming.' The lesson which our Lord taught he practised. We read throughout the New Testament of his spending whole nights in prayer, doubtless for us sinners, and likewise for support from his heavenly Father to himself in his human capacity. That awful and solemn scene in the

garden of Gethsemane is an example of the most
striking kind to us of the necessity of prayer. So,
if the holy, sinless Saviour prayed for support, how
much more should we !

Again, Paul tells us to 'come boldly to the
throne of grace, that we may obtain mercy.' Be-
siege, then, God's throne with supplications for
mercy. Pray not once nor coldly, but beseech
God to save your soul, as you would entreat a
mortal to stretch out his hand to you if you were
dying. We are told that Christ Jesus, whilst on
this earth, 'offered up prayers and supplications,
with strong crying and tears.' Every converted
man has more or less done the same. Do not
think God is indifferent because an answer does
not come immediately. God answers prayer in
his way, not in ours. The answer has often come
before it was recognised, the shape was so different from what was expected. You have many
mercies ; thank God for them ; and if you doubt
that he will reply to your requests, then pray for
faith to believe that he will. However dark and
anguished your thoughts may be, let not go hold

of God's mercy. Say, if you can say no more, with Job, 'Though he slay me, yet will I trust in him.' Pray, D., and read God's Word, and fear not that the answer and the blessing will be sent.

Forgive this scrawl. I will write at length on Sabbath.

December 19*th*, 1847.

DEAR FRIEND,—I have been dwelling in the last two hurried letters on the immense importance of diligently reading the Word of God, and of being earnest in prayer. The former is spoken of as the 'sword of the Spirit.' It is the weapon which the Holy Ghost most frequently employs in the conversion of sinners. When you are reading it, you are, as it were, baring your bosom to the sword of God, which smites to heal ; and then, my friend, I cannot too often urge on you the value and importance of prayer. It is an instrument, as it were, which God has put into our hands, and told us to use, as a means of bringing down blessings upon us. If we use it in the appointed way, the blessing will not be denied ; if we despise or neglect it, we shall not only miss the blessing, but receive the curse. Men who do not understand in the slightest, the construction of the electric telegraph, have yet faith in what its constructors have told them of its power to convey messages and bring back replies, and show their faith by using it. Prayer is a much more marvellous engine, and if men would only believe this and employ it, even half as trustingly as they do a telegraph, the increase of happiness they would receive is incalculable. But we are all (amazing sin and folly!) more willing to believe what the most worthless fellow-being tells us than to credit God's declarations.

To pray to God is a very solemn act. It is asking an infinitely holy being, the King eternal, immortal, and invisible, to turn aside from his omnipotent doings, and listen to a single sinner. God's eye is always on us, but here we are beseeching him to fix it upon us. A holy creature would pray to God with the greatest solemnity. How much more, then, should a sinful creature tremble to enter into the presence of God! We all forget this too much. Man's sin and folly is most conspicuous in the indifference with which he approaches God. With what feelings of awe would any of us enter the presence of the Queen, or of the Duke of Wellington, or of the distinguished men of science and letters who are the objects of our regard and admiration. We would be all anxiety to show our deference, most desirous to express our sense of the greatness of the persons before us, very solicitous to make a favourable impression and not to appear devoid of true humility, or presumptuous. Yet from the presence of earthly greatness men will pass to that of the King of kings, and then in some hasty, formal way, utter with scanty reverence, a thoughtless prayer, and depart thankful that an irksome task is over. My friend, so long as we pray thus, we pray in vain. We do worse, we are bringing down coals of fire upon our heads.

The Bible-scheme of prayer is, I think, that we ask God the Father to forgive us our sins, for the sake of his Son, and to grant us the Holy Spirit to sanctify us. I do not think we are for-

bidden to address each person of the Trinity, and
good men in all ages have prayed to each. The
Father is the representative of the Godhead in the
Trinity, and as such is generally addressed in the
prayers recorded in the New Testament. But all
Christian prayer must be regarded as addressed to
the whole Trinity, whichever person be named,
for all must consent before a soul can be saved.
When you address God, therefore, my dear friend,
keep thoughtfully in mind that in so doing, you
are beseeching the Father to forgive you, sinful as
you are, because Christ offered up a sacrifice of
infinite value, a 'propitiation for the sins of the
whole world,' and therefore for yours, so that as
he was counted guilty, and suffered in the room
of the guilty, dying the just for the unjust, you,
one of the unjust and the guilty, may have his
righteousness imputed to you, and for his sake be
counted holy. In Christian prayer, you are also
entreating the Son to be your advocate with the
Father, and to make intercession for you, as one
whose advocacy and intercession are all-prevailing. You are likewise imploring the Holy Spirit

to intercede for you with the Father and Son, and to sanctify your requests, and make them acceptable. Such is Christian prayer; not the cold utterance of a formal request to an unknown, awful power; but the outpouring of a broken heart and a contrite spirit, before the long-suffering, covenant-keeping God and Father of our Lord Jesus Christ.

When I was recovering from the loss of my foot, you can well believe that there were many weary, wretched, sleepless hours, particularly during darkness. Especially dreary was the first waking in the dull, grey morning. Despair seemed ready to overwhelm me. It was then I fully realized the unspeakable preciousness of prayer, and that not to an overwhelming mysterious agency, such as electricity or gravitation is, but to an *Agent*, a *Person*, and he not separated from me by all that intervenes between God and man, but possessing, as I possess, a human nature; though, unlike mine, His nature is sinless, and is unspeakably glorious. It would be no comfort to think that His nature was sinful, or corruptible; that would lower Christ to me, not lift me to him.　Here was the precious thought,—' We have not an high priest which cannot be touched with the feeling of our infirmities ; but was in all points tempted [or tried] like as we are, yet without sin.'　There was no kind of trial I had, or you have, which Christ had not; he could understand it from a fellow-feeling as man, apart from discerning it as omniscient God.　He heard my prayers ; he loved me with his great love ; and his good Spirit reminded me that the Saviour said, ' Lo, I am with you alway.'　And he is as willing to be your Saviour as to be mine.　In the Epistle I have been quoting, we are told that Jesus put on a human nature that he might suffer death,—the object of this suffering being ' that he, by the grace of God, should taste death for every man.'　You have the fear of death and of judgment before you. Christ died, ' that through death, he might destroy him that had the power of death, that is, the devil, and deliver them who, through fear of death, were all their lifetime subject to bondage.'

Think, my dear friend, of Christ as an Elder Brother, gazing down from heaven with more than

an earthly brother's love. Think of him also as
divinely omnipotent, and 'able to save them to the
uttermost that come unto God by him, seeing he
ever liveth to make intercession for them,' and go
to the throne of grace, asking for mercy and forgiveness. Wait not till you love the world less,
and hate sin more. God will not accept you because you hate the world or sin. Between your
great lovings of the world and your little ones,
there will never be much more than an insignificant difference. Even your own heart tells you
that; much more does God know it. The only
wages man can ever earn, and ask from God as
his of right, are the wages of sin, *i.e.*, death.
Eternal life is the *gift* of God. Make no conditions with God, or think to recommend yourself to
him by wishes or merits. Far less wait till you realize, if possible, recommendatory merits, or despair
because these merits are not realized. Go with
all your sins without a moment's waiting. Go as
a sinner, and because you are a sinner. Christ
'came not to call the righteous, but sinners to repentance.' It was not while we were righteous,

but 'whilst we were yet in our sins, Christ died for us.' 'Herein is love; not that we loved God, but that he loved us, and sent him to be the propitiation for our sins.' 'We love him, because he first loved us.'

The conditions God imposes on you are simply these,—'If we confess our sins, he is faithful and just to forgive us our sins, and to cleanse us from all unrighteousness.'

Make it a great point to study the character of Christ in one of the Gospels, and then in some of the Epistles. You cannot well go wrong anywhere. Luke is the fullest history. John is the deepest in unfolding our Saviour's inner nature. The Epistle to the Hebrews is most consecutive in argument, and complete in itself; Romans is more difficult. Read what you like best, praying for the Holy Spirit to guide you into an understanding of its meaning. The Holy Spirit is the author of the Bible. He only can tell us its full meaning, and open our carnal eyes to perceive its spiritual lessons. You will not labour in vain; God is a prayer-answering God, and will send you a reply.

Tell me your difficulties, and I will do what I can to help you ; but look to God, not to men, for light and assistance.

Your sincerely attached.

December 23d, 1847.

DEAR FRIEND,—I have read with feelings of the greatest delight, as you will readily believe, your last two letters. You are now able, with more or less confidence, to say, Whereas I was blind, now I see : ' The darkness is past, and the true light now shineth.' Yet, my friend, wonder not if you are not able to see Life and Death, Time and Eternity, in all points, fully revealed in the unshadowed meridian blaze of his teaching, who is ' light, and in whom is no darkness at all.' Rejoice that the night of spiritual darkness is not only far spent with you, and the day of Christian enlightenment at hand, but that the day *hath* dawned, and the day-star arisen in your heart ; and ' walk in the light,' doubting not that the Lord Jesus Christ, who ' dwelleth in the light which no man can approach unto,' will, if you walk in the light as he is in the light, cleanse you from all sin.

Remember that even when we become new creatures in Christ, through the regenerating power of the Holy Spirit, and are able, through the spirit of adoption, to look up to God, not as a mere Ruler, Governor, and Master, but as a reconciled God and Father, we are not released from the influence of habit, or in a moment made to understand all mysteries of a spiritual kind, and all knowledge. The heart, long and resolutely closed against the entrance of holiness, and which God has quite recently opened by his irresistible grace, cannot in an instant of time be filled with the fulness of him that filleth all in all. It will take nothing less than eternity to do that. Old habits cannot in a moment be changed, or ignorance at once replaced by perfect knowledge. The saints of the Old Testament, and the very apostles of the New, were long and patiently instructed by the Spirit of God, but even those whom Christ himself taught, and to whom the Spirit was given in unusual measure, learned only very slowly the deep things of God; and one of the greatest of them, Paul, said in his own name, and in that of all his fellow-Christians, 'We know in part, and we prophesy in part.' You will find Paul's estimate of himself more explicitly stated in Philippians iii. 12-14; and how he thought of his own great faith, when he compared it with what it might be, and what he knew it would be in heaven.

Above all, think of this, that all Scripture is given by inspiration, and that all of it is 'profitable for instruction.' Till it has been better studied, we must not and cannot wonder if our religious faith and belief are weak and imperfect. Your own conscience will tell you, as mine tells me, that it is not because we do not know *all* the Bible, but because we scarcely know any of it, that we make so slow progress in the Christian life. God is not superfluous of means. He has, in his providence, given you and me a Bible, and he will not reveal to us by any other media what he has told us there. Let not, therefore, the feeling of imperfect knowledge of Christ, and corresponding weakness of faith, be met by mere lamentation over our ignorance. He who

has given us a little faith will give us a great
deal, if we will use the means he has afforded
for the purpose. Prayer is the one ; the reading
of God's Word is the other. It is useless to ask
God to give us more light, when we are not
making use of the torch of revelation he has put
in our hands. Therefore, my beloved friend,
fail not, whilst you lament your ignorance, to set
about its instant removal, by a deeper study of
God's dealings toward man, and his revelation of
his will as given in his Word.

On other matters I will trouble you with a
word. Do not distress yourself because your
faith is not always equally clear and strong. It
is not so with any Christian, far less is it so with
one like you, just 'passed from darkness to light.'
God's Spirit is not given even to his saints in
the same measure at all times : Satan tempts
more at one time than at another : lawful occupations, unavoidable duties, and unexpected occur-
rences, and the like, disturb, engage, or ruffle our
hearts with an influence by no means uniform :
the state of our health is a powerful additional

cause of fluctuation in our spiritual feelings, and so also is the constitution of our individual minds. It is vain, therefore, to expect to have one uniform mood of religious faith. So long as our consciences and the Holy Spirit do not tell us that the cause of our declension in faith is an act of sin, we distrust God if we fall into doubt or despair. Yet in all cases the remedy is the same. It lies not in curiously and tremblingly watching the rise and fall of the spiritual thermometer in our hearts, nor in fixing our despairing eyes on it when it has gone down to zero. If we have sinned, the cure lies in instantly flying to God's throne and beseeching forgiveness, and we shall never go wrong in doing so; and next in dwelling on the only thing that can strengthen our faith, namely, the fulness and freeness of God's offer of salvation to us through the unspeakable gift of his dear Son, and the certainty of his willingness to hear and answer all earnest Christian prayer, and to help us by his Holy Spirit.

Secondly, do not wonder and lament if you cannot see that your present afflicted state is the

best one for you.   Many good people make the
mistake of insisting on sufferers acknowledging
that their miseries are in *all* respects blessings,
which they should thank God for as such : God,
who knoweth our frames, has not asked this at
our hands.   It is arrogating to ourselves the
Lord's prerogative of omniscience to pretend to
affirm that we *see* that what has happened to us
is the best thing that could have happened.   An
affliction would be no trial of our faith if we saw
this.   Now, it is an essential condition of our
probation here that we should walk by faith, *not
by sight;* that we should *not see* that what happens is best, but should believe *without* seeing,
or having proof offered us, that it is best, simply
because God has ordained it.   I do not pretend to have perceived that my illnesses were the
best things that could have occurred to me : I
am content to rejoice in the conviction that ' *all*
things work together for good' to God's people.
Assuredly I see *good;* but I do not venture to
say that I see *best:* it is enough to see the former.   Shall not you and I, my friend, thank our

blessed Lord and Master, through all eternity, that he sent us illness, when he blessed that to effect what health had not brought about, namely, our recognition of his love and mercy even to us?

Here is abounding cause of unceasing thankfulness. It is enough to have this to praise God for. He may show us in another world that it was not only good, but best for us to bear the yoke he laid on us. Meanwhile, he tries our faith by giving us no proof, of what we may well believe, that all was very good; and he stills our murmurs by saying, as he did to Paul, 'My grace is sufficient for you: my strength is made perfect in weakness.' The Lord answer our prayers, and thus reveal himself to you and your affectionate friend.

January 28th, 1848.

DEAR D.,—I hoped to have seen you before this, or I would have answered your letter on Monday. . . . . As for the hydrogen speculation, that can best be talked over. This much, how-

ever, may be said. If I spoke of hydrogen as
the acidifier, it was not as the utterance of a
special opinion of mine, but as the prevailing
chemical doctrine; neither did I desire to recommend that hydrogen should have changed its
name into *oxygen.* What I have been in the
habit of saying has been to the effect, that if
the *system* of nomenclature which introduced the
terms oxygen, hydrogen, etc., were retained, but
the names given anew, hydrogen would (not
should) be called oxygen, and oxygen, Basigen;
but I did not recommend that such names should
be given. The import of the statement was, or
intended to be, that as the majority of chemists
regard hydrogen as the acidifier, they would, if
they called any body oxygen, give that title to
hydrogen. I am quite disposed to agree with
you in thinking that no one body can be entitled
to the name of '*the* oxygen,' or 'the acidifier,' as if
there were no other substance able to confer acidity upon its compounds. I am afraid, however,
that I must dissent from your belief, that prepond-
erance of non-metallic ingredient in a compound

is sufficient to confer upon the latter acidity. If this view were correct, should not all per-chlorides, iodides, bromides, sulphurets, etc., be acids? Yet there is (*e.g.*) a penta-sulphuret of potassium, basic rather than acid. Before, however, we could discuss this topic, we should require to settle what the definition of an acid, a salt, etc., was; all which matters can much better be talked over at length when we meet, than be made the subject of brief letters. We shall, therefore, if you please, adjourn the discussion. Some experiments which I have been making since last summer, on the action of colouring matter on the dry gases, promise to throw light on this question of acids, and their relation to hydrogen. You shall see these trials in progress when you come.

Meanwhile, forgive the brevity of this note. I have not, for the last three weeks, known what it was to find a quiet moment: I shall make up to you by and by for my recent deficiencies. Praying God to bless and guide, instruct and save you, I remain,

Your affectionate friend.

February 20th, 1848.

DEAR D.,—You must excuse my delay in writing. If you would but help me with a sugges-
tion — if you would offer even a hint as to the
points on which we might exchange thoughts,
I should be able, with the sense that I was discussing relevant matter, to write at least cordially
and heartily; whereas, left by you free to write
on anything, I know not what to write. My
letter becomes a vague sermon, instead of a
genial epistle. Ignorant of your bodily state, and
unable to guess what subjects you would suggest,
if we were conversing together, I feel that, the
talk being all on my side, I am likely only to
tire you, or to discuss what, lying at present out
of the range of your sympathy, is not a subject
of interest to you. To you only can I look for
help, and you can furnish it without invading on
the privacy or sacredness of your own thoughts.
We are both satisfied that the mere revelation of
our own thoughts will supply far too slender a
subject for a continuous correspondence. Well,

then, let a scriptural doctrine be talked over between us, as some chemical doctrines have been. There need be no *confession* on either side, but only grave statement of opinion; and if you and I discuss it with as much earnestness as we do our favourite notions on chemistry, I doubt not that, with the help of God's good Spirit, it will redound to our edification. I shall willingly, as (*ex hypothesi*) the healthier man (?), take the lion's share in the discussion as long as I can, unless you relieve me; but you must *say something.* Letter for letter must be the terms; only the scantiest scrap shall be accepted, and counted worth much.

I begin then by enclosing you the accompanying paper,[1] of which only twenty copies have been reprinted for my very particular friends. It is mainly occupied with the consideration of the meaning of suffering in this world. The subject cannot but interest a sufferer like you, whatever you think of the argument, and perhaps it may help you to increased patience under your

[1] 'Chemistry and Natural Theology.'

trials. The conviction that this earth has, since it became habitable, always been the abode of sufferers, may well close your lips and mine, when we selfishly complain that our brethren are well, and we alone marked out for misery. Those who, like us, are well enough to mix with the quite well, but too ill to run the race of life on equal terms with them, are particularly apt, as I find at least in my case, to repine. We grudge them their health, and count it a singularly hard thing that on us affliction should have fallen. Nature even reproaches us for this. The dead pre-Adamite dragons and fossil monsters reprove us for our guilt and folly. The very stones cry out against us.

The lesson from nature is worth learning, but it does not teach much after all. The consciousness that our dearest friend is a sufferer does not lessen our agonies, much less the forgotten pangs of extinct animals. It may lead us with more reverence than before to *the* Great Sufferer. Nature, with a sad countenance, excuses herself from explaining the mystery of suffering, but takes us by the hand,

and leading us to the cross of Christ, bids us ask its meaning from him who was 'made perfect through sufferings.' And the glorified Saviour, now 'a Lamb that *was* slain,' replies, 'Come unto me, and I will give you rest; I am not a High Priest that cannot be touched with the feeling of your infirmities. I was tried and tempted in all points like as you are, though without sin; and inasmuch as I have suffered, being tried, I am able to succour you when you are tempted or tried.'

We are dictating terms to God if we demand health from him; we are denying his justice and his omniscience, for we are assuming, either that he refuses what he knows to be best for us, or that he is not aware that it is best.

The essence of all Christian prayer, on the other hand, is that clause of our Lord's Prayer, 'Thy will be done on earth as it is in heaven.' Our Saviour, when he endured the mysterious, but awful, unspeakably tremendous agony in the garden, besought that the still greater, and to us inconceivable sufferings that were to follow, might be spared him ; but he added, whilst addressing this request to his heavenly Father, ' Nevertheless, thy will be done.' By precept and by example, we are taught ever to pray in the spirit of entire submission to the Divine will. We are to make our wants known : to ask assuagement of suffering is a Christian prayer ; but to ask *nothing* but that, is an unsanctified and unhallowed petition.

God has promised us something far better than health, namely, that all things shall work together for good to those who love God. It is promised that the present afflictions, though not joyous but grievous, afterwards redound to the greater happiness of those who are reconciled to God.

We, the weary and the heavy laden, shall, if we walk worthy of our calling, very soon carry no other than the quite tolerable burden ' of an exceeding and *eternal* WEIGHT of glory.'

Have you recently read the 12th of Hebrews? The book of Job and the Hebrews should lie on each sick man's pillow.

With much love and sympathy, yours affection-
ately.

February 27th, 1848.

DEAR D.,—The love of God is a thing so delightful to dwell upon, and one the study of which
is so certain to profit us, that I feel glad you have
suggested it as a topic for our consideration.

I will begin by saying that I think the statement of the apostle John that ' God is love,' does
not appear to have been intended immediately to
refer to the elect or the non-elect, the regenerate
or the unregenerate. It is a simple affirmation of
a quality of God's nature, which exists irrespec-
tively of his creatures ; which belonged to the
Eternal before man was created, or fell, and would
remain although creation were annihilated. There
is a manifest distinction between the extent to
which it may become apparent or be developed to
us. God's love is infinite in its nature, or extent,
or essence ; but it does not follow that the degree
to which it shall be manifested to his creatures must be unlimited. It is in the *extent* to

which God *manifests* his love, that there is a difference between his dealings towards the regenerate and unregenerate. 'He is the same
yesterday, to-day, and for ever' to both, so far
as the unchangeableness of his perfect being is
concerned. We must not allow any difficulties
in the way of reconciling God's attributes with
his dealings, to lead us to infringe on the infinite-
ness of the former. If we speak of God's love
as limited, it must be only in reference to its
manifestation, not to its nature. Why a God who
is all-loving, should show more love to some of
his creatures than to others is to us a great mystery, a problem utterly insoluble to human reason.
Your solution is of a different problem, for it
denies that God is all-loving; whereas the question is, Given a God who is love, to reconcile this
with the suffering of certain of his creatures : this
your reply does not touch.

I must further add that it is *not* a Scriptural
doctrine that God shows love only to the regenerate. My dear friend, only consider to whom the
wicked are indebted for life, health, food, raiment,

temporal comforts, domestic happiness, social joys, intellectual and moral gratifications, etc. etc., and can you doubt that God is love, even to the most thankless, ignorant, and sinful of his creatures? The Bible is very plain on this point. Christ declared that God 'maketh his sun to rise on the evil and the good, and sendeth rain on the just and the unjust.' Again, 'He is kind to the unthankful and the evil.' Think of that amazing expression of love, even towards his murderers, which proceeded from the lips of him who spake as never man spake : 'Father, forgive them, for they know not what they do !' In the first chapter of Proverbs, from the twentieth verse onwards, the strongest expressions of love, interest, earnest entreaty, and affectionate beseeching, are addressed even to the despisers of God's love, for whom punishment is preparing. In the second chapter of Romans occurs this passage : 'Despisest thou the riches of his goodness, and forbearance, and long-suffering ; not knowing that the goodness of God leadeth thee to repentance? But after thy hardness and impenitent heart treasurest up unto thyself wrath, against the day of wrath and revelation of the righteous judgment of God.' Here the unregenerate are reproached for despising the love shown to them by God.

No one is a firmer believer in the doctrine of election than I am, but we are not—because we cannot reconcile a free offer of the gospel to all with an actual acceptance of it only by a few, and a certain punishment of those who reject it—to tamper with God's attributes, or speak of his love as limited only to the elect. It is their inestimable privilege, to which I pray God may exalt us both, to be the peculiar objects of his unspeakable love, but love is not forgotten in his manifestations to any of his creatures. Let us think of that plain passage, 'God's tender mercies are over all his works.' The lost spirits in hell, and the fallen angels—although the thought of God as love is perhaps the bitterest drop in their cup of agony, as reminding them that they have lost the favour of the most benignant of beings—stand, I doubt not, indebted even to that love. Their punishment is greater than they can bear, awful to think of, yet it is much less than God's justice entitled, and infinitely less than his justice enabled him to inflict.

Let us adore and exalt God in all his manifestations, magnify his name and make it honourable, bow ourselves beneath his will, and he will exalt us in due time.

I would add a word more, lest you are liable, as I have been—and sufferers as a class are likely to be—to exaggerate God's love at the expense of his other attributes. The assurance that God is love does not imply that he is all-love, *i.e.*, that he is nothing but love, neither does it in the least imply that love is the highest of his attributes. Yet I think we are very apt to dwell with much complacency upon God's goodness, mercy, and compassion, from which we anticipate relief to our sufferings, but are far less willing to dwell upon his justice, and least of all, on his holiness. Nevertheless, God is not more the All-loving than he is the All-just and the All-holy; and a faith which should seek to evade this, and endeavour to build upon the infinite love alone, or should seek to give the latter more prominence than the former, would, when tried by the fire, burn away like stubble. No subtle metaphysics are needed to demonstrate this great truth. When God's mighty love came forth to save fallen man, it did not come forth alone; side by side advanced his inflexible justice and spotless holiness, each with claims upon God as great as his love. Read the proof of this in the life and death of Christ. The 'Father loveth the Son,' as he loveth none else, but his justice did not fail to exact to the very uttermost the penalty due to his broken law from him who in his unspeakable love 'bare our sins in his own body on the tree,' and God's holiness remained, as it were, in abeyance, so far as man was concerned, till the risen Saviour appeared as 'a Lamb that *was* slain,' and sat down at the right hand of the Majesty on high. Then only was the Comforter sent, the Holy Spirit, to make men holy.

The same justice that relented not towards the sinless Saviour when he was made sin for us, is still inflexible in its demands on us. The same holiness declares, 'Be ye holy, for I am holy.' Without holiness no man shall see the Lord.

To be certain, then, that we have an interest in Christ's blood, so that when God's justice demands atonement for our breaches of his righteous law to be made by *our* suffering punishment, or another for us, we may be able to point to the blessed Saviour as our surety and advocate with the Father, is as essential as to know that God is love. And equally essential is it that we have been born again, and sanctified by the Holy Spirit. The cultivation, indeed, of personal holiness, and of a closer hold upon Christ, a greater right through faith, and power to call him our Elder Brother, are duties, if possible, lying nearer us than the mere contemplation of God's love. Every sin we commit, every departure from holiness, drives, as it were, to a distance from us God's love; nor will it return till obedience, repentance, and holiness do. How solemn are the warnings in the Bible! 'Make your calling and election sure.' 'Work out your salvation with fear and trembling.'

Above all, let us avoid thinking of our sufferings as something that deserves compensation, or of heaven merely as a place of reward. The lowest of all motives that can influence a man to do his manifest and unquestionable duty, is the promise of a reward for doing what he ought to be punished for not doing. Yet men are too apt to think of the joys of heaven, and to forget the conditions of tasting them. It is promised to the Christian that he shall receive 'the end of his faith, the salvation of his soul.' The faith is first, however. We are not to be made happy in heaven as one thing, and holy as another. We are to be made happy solely because we are holy, made like unto God, through Christ, and happy in degree as he is infinitely happy, because we are holy in degree, as he is altogether.

April 30th, 1848.

Dear D.,—I did not anticipate, when last I wrote to you, that so long a time was to elapse before I should write again. Unusual occupation, illness in our household, and, latterly, indisposition as affecting myself, have prevented me sending so much as a line. I quite counted on writing to you both last Sabbath and the one before, but I was too ill to attempt it. I am better now, though utterly worn out with my winter's work, and thankful to rest from labour.

Here is the last day of Spring, and to-morrow, according to the almanacs, Summer — a blessed word for invalids—begins. The real summer, however, I fear, is much farther off, and a trying season for all valetudinarians must be passed through before genial weather comes. I have learned by many a painful lesson that it is folly to build our hopes on any secondary sources of happiness. Seasons of the year can, of themselves, neither harm nor profit us; and all seasons are in God's hand, and will affect us for good or ill only as he pleases. It is hard to learn this lesson of entire faith in God, and perfect submission to his will. I am a poor scholar at it, and make slow progress; but the lesson must be learned, cost what it may. Submit we must, willingly or unwillingly : if willingly, there is a promise that, if we humble ourselves before the mighty God, he will exalt us in due time.

I do not attempt to take up our correspondence

at the point where it dropped, for probably your points of interest and difficulty have altered greatly since then. I remember, however, that you referred to the sixth chapter of Hebrews, and, as I gathered, especially to the fourth and immediately succeeding verses. The doctrine of 'assurance of salvation,' as it has been called, or as it is also named, that of the 'perseverance of the saints,' is a plain doctrine of the Bible, and must, I think, be held by every one who believes the doctrine of election; but we must be careful what use we make of it. God has not promised to any of his people an *absolute* assurance, in the way of a specific communication that their salvation is inevitable ; and if you read the diaries of the holiest Christians, you will find everything rather than exultations that they are his elect. What God has done is to give every man simple and easily applied tests, by which he may discover whether he is one of his people or not. Day by day the test is to be applied; for it does not directly signify what a man's condition will be on the morrow, although indirectly it has the most important bearing on his future, as well as on his present condition. The test, or rather tests, are these,—Love to God and love to man. Stated more fully, we are to ask ourselves, Do we hate sin and avoid it? do we love God and holiness? do we love Christ, and feel delight in serving and obeying him? do we entreat for the Holy Spirit, and submit to his guidance? If we can say 'yea' and 'amen' to these questions, we have the witness of the Spirit that we are God's and not Satan's servants; that we are Christ's, not our own. Yet do not, my dear friend, forget that the Christian life is a progressive thing. Regeneration, which is the Spirit's work, begins the new life; sanctification, which is also his work, continues it. The moment a man is born again, he is safe, so that if he died that moment he would go to heaven; but if he continued on this earth, he will not halt at the point of *birth*, and remain ever a babe in grace,—he will 'grow in grace;' become more and more deeply versed in God's law; better and better acquainted with his will; more jealous of sin, and more successful in overcoming it; holier in act and thought; more devotedly attached to his Lord and Master,

Christ Jesus, till he come, in the unity of the faith
and of the knowledge of the Son of God, unto a perfect man, unto the measure of the stature of the
fulness of Christ.' The infants that go to heaven
are doubtless carried through stages of progression
also, and rise from strength to strength till they
are made ' meet for the inheritance of the saints in
light.' I have often thought that Jacob's dream of
the ladder, by which the angels ascended and de-
scended, was intended to teach the same or a
similar lesson. Heaven is not to be won at a
bound ; we are not in a moment to become holy
as God is holy. Up a long and toilsome ladder
must most of us climb, not without frequent slip-
pings back, and loss of ground, mounting slowly,
often sadly, to the gate of heaven. Think how
even the holy Paul counted not himself to have
already attained, or to be already perfect, but forgetting those things which were before, pressed
toward the mark of the prize of the high calling of
God in Christ Jesus. In this fine allusion to the
foot-races of the Grecian games, we have a most
instructive and encouraging lesson. I do not

gather from your letters, nor should I judge from
your temperament, especially as affected by ill
health, that your temptation is towards counting
yourself spiritually perfect. But I think that you
do not imitate the Apostle in forgetting the things
that are behind, and that you give yourself, in consequence, pain which might be avoided, as well as
thwart your spiritual progress. Do not, my dear
friend, imagine that I say this harshly or dogmati-
cally, or with the purpose of fastening on you a
heavy charge. I know that I may be quite un-
warranted in what I am urging, and I crave you
to forgive me if I am. Unwise retrospect is, however, so common an error of even Christians
far advanced in the heavenly life, that I can
scarcely be altogether wrong in imputing it to
you. It is a thing that human weakness can
scarcely avoid, without neglecting (which were a
greater sin) the duty of self-examination and revi-
sion of the past. Yet, if we are to look back only
to lament, as now unattainable, states of religious
feeling or spiritual experience which once were
ours ; or to despair over the past as black with

F

unpardonable sins, we are also sinning grievously
and acting unwisely, for we always colour the past,
especially the far distant past, and make it blacker
or brighter than, as the present, it was. If our
past religious attainments had been achieved by
our own unaided efforts, we might have some
ground for affirming that never again should we
be able to reach to the spiritual heights which
we once climbed, and ought now, if making progress in the divine life, to be leaving below us.
But if it were God that led us, the blind, by
a way we knew not, and made crooked places
straight, and rough places plain before us : and
the Holy Spirit, that convinced us of sin, and
made us new creatures in Christ; and if it were
Christ's strength that was made perfect in our
weakness, then, unless they have changed and
grown powerless, we shall still find their 'grace
sufficient for us.'

God, moreover, has revealed to no man that he
has been guilty of the unpardonable sin, or that
he is beyond grace. On the other hand, he has
proclaimed in letters of light and love that he

desireth not the death of the wicked, that Christ
died for the chief of sinners, and that he is a
propitiation for the sins of the whole world.   It
is despising the mercy and forbearance of God,
to doubt or forget this ; and what, my dear friend,
if, whilst we are lamenting that we have fallen
from high attainments, the real state of matters
was, that we had but scanty spiritual graces to
fall from.   I desire not to write as if the loss of
these was not deeply to be lamented, or as if
our backslidings were to be made light of to ourselves, or regarded as light in the eye of God.
They are to be repented in dust and ashes ; we
are to implore our heavenly Father to forgive
them : we are to consider them as warning us
to 'watch' and to 'pray' more than ever against
being led into temptation.   Yet despair, one of
the offspring of Satan and sin, is to be driven
away by the cheering remembrance that there is
one who was manifested 'that he might destroy
the works of the devil,' and who has led 'cap-
tivity captive,' and 'spoiled principalities and
powers, making a show of them openly.'   We

are to rejoice in the assurance that 'if any man sin, we have an Advocate with the Father, Jesus Christ the righteous.'

Let this further be remembered, that if you cannot abidingly realize the '*full* assurance' of faith at all times, but have alternations of great trust, and of little confidence; now welcoming the Spirit's witnessing with your spirit that you love Christ, now despairing of making your calling and election sure : if this be the case, do not forget that it is no uncommon case. These are not necessarily unbecoming accompaniments of Christian experience. For historical proof of this, look to the penitential psalms of David, and to the almost despair of the suffering Job ; to Paul contemplating as possible his being a cast-away, and Peter writing 'If the righteous scarcely be saved, where shall the ungodly and the sinner appear ?' Think of all this, and do not write a sentence of condemnation against yourself, till you have exhausted (?) the inexhaustible grace of our Saviour.

All the saints I have named were, even after

their calling by God, sinners in the eye of him, of man, even of themselves,—some of them sinned grievously,—but they were forgiven for Christ's sake, when with strong crying and tears they besieged the throne of grace ; and Christ, their Christ and our Christ, the same yesterday, to-day, and for ever, ' ever liveth to make intercession for us.' It is true that God's forgiveness of backsliders has been, and is liable to be, greatly abused on the plea, that as God's elect can never fall, any sins they may commit will certainly be forgiven them. I do not think that this statement goes beyond what is implied in the Bible. Oliver Cromwell applied to himself as a ground of hope the striking words, ' Once in grace, always in grace.' I make no objections to the words as expressing a truth, a very cheering Christian truth. This, however, as I have probably sufficiently indicated at the beginning, is not the test by which God desires or permits us to try the reality of our faith ; and if too much dwelt upon, to the exclusion of other Bible truths, is apt to lead to the inference so fatal to all godliness, that we may sin because grace abounds. But unless we are wilfully and deliberately sinning, and of purpose 'turning the grace of God into lasciviousness,' on the plea that we certainly are the elect, this is not the transgression that we require most to avoid. In all respects strait is the road and narrow is the way that leadeth unto life eternal. There is sinful confidence on the one side, and sinful despair on the other, and either may tempt us and drag us into the broad road that leadeth to destruction. But there is one mode of avoiding both these, and all other temptations to desert the path of life. Christ trod it all before us, and the prints of his footsteps are visible to those eyes which the Holy Spirit has opened; and our Saviour retraces the road with every one of his people; with his rod and staff comforts them; and is with them always even to the end.

You will find much to suit your case in the epistles of that chief apostle and holy man Peter, who knew what it was to fall. I refer especially to the beginning of each epistle. In the second, at the tenth verse of the first chapter, after enumerating many graces as yet attainable or improvable, even by the Christian, he adds, ' If ye do these things, ye shall never fall.' Connect with this Paul's declaration, ' I can do all things, Christ strengthening me,' as the prerogative of every Christian, and I will end, my dear friend, by commending you 'unto him that is able to *keep you from falling,* and to present you faultless before the presence of his glory with exceeding joy.' Amen.

LETTERS TO MRS Y.

DEAR MRS. Y.,—I read with great sorrow your letter received this morning, filled as it is with mournful details. I have always fancied that if I were a parent I should feel the illness of children a greater cause of distress than almost anything else. I think I should prefer suffering myself to seeing them suffer. Poor G.[1] I will be the last, my dear friend, to blame you, if you feel your faith and patience sometimes strained almost past endurance, when you see the little fellow aching over the unbroken monotony and irksomeness of his position. I know by experience how much unsuspected physical misery is

---

[1] An invalid boy, son of Mrs. Y.

occasioned by lying for hours in one constrained posture. With G., therefore, I can and do sympathize very heartily.

As for trust in almighty power and kindness, it would be a mournful thing if we lost faith in that. I hope, however, you do not imagine I suppose that a painful event like G.'s illness can be made a joyful one, if our trust in God can be sufficient; and that I shall blame you if it never lose its character of painfulness in relation to you.

I do not think the Bible anywhere professes to blame us for feeling pain, sickness, poverty, and the like, as distresses. On the other hand, it plainly declares that 'no affliction for the present is joyous, but grievous.' It is a moral, not a physical, triumph we are promised over physical ills. Pain is as acute to a devout Christian, poverty as hard to bear, disappointment as painful, so far as they are considered alone, as they can be to the careless or profane. There is no exemption on these points, for the Christian.

To profess, moreover, to discover what God's

object was in sending us particular afflictions, must, in the great majority of cases, be an unwise occupation ; although not always. But I think we may always find something to learn from what happens to us; and that if we have some profitable lesson taught it is enough, without insisting that that lesson, and no other, was the one intended to be taught.

I myself have felt, for example, when ill, a sense of dependence on God, and nearness to him, which I have seldom realized so powerfully when in health. I have also in such circumstances, when all worldly and ordinary occupations were felt to be impossible, had a relish for reading the Bible, and a profit in perusing it, such as I experienced at no other times. I might refer to other things, but I only wish to illustrate that to get good out of sorrow is the great matter, without affirming that we are getting all the good and the intended good from it.

I think in the present case, if you will forgive a solicitude prompted only by friendship, I should deem it a great point to instil into G.'s mind the conviction that he is in the hands of God. I should inculcate patience, on the ground that he cannot suffer to any such extent as Christ did when upon this earth, and teach him to pray for patience to Him 'who can be touched with a feeling of our infirmities,' and who, inasmuch as he hath suffered, being tempted (or tried), is able to succour us when we are tempted. It is a great sweetener of the temper, a great help through the long and weary hours of sickness, to believe that there is in heaven one cognisant of our condition, and both willing and able to send us help. Into the mind of one so young as G., such a thought can easily be introduced. Night and morning some little simple prayer might be uttered by him, made up of a few sentences, chiefly from the Bible. It would slowly sink into the heart.

And in addition to that, I am a great advocate for surrounding the sick with pleasant things—flowers, pictures, toys. You well remember the extraordinary progress Sir W. Scott made when lying in bed, a little lame boy. There is great encouragement in that.   A companion of G.'s own age to play at draughts, backgammon, or chess, with him, would be a great matter with a boy so amiable.   I should hope that the weary bed-riddenness might be much alleviated in various ways. My love to him.   .   .   .

January 18th, 1848.

DEAR MRS. Y.,—I have read your letter with feelings of the deepest Christian sympathy and interest, and I shall truly rejoice if I can help you, however imperfectly, over any of the difficulties that lie in your way.   Assuredly I shall consider this no trouble, but a great pleasure ; a plain duty, for we are to ' bear each other's burdens, and so fulfil the law of Christ ;' and one to which a great blessing is attached, inasmuch as it is promised that ' he that watereth others shall himself be watered.'   Only the last assurance strengthens me to take upon myself the otherwise presumptuous office of seeming to teach any one the deep things of God.   I am in these things but a child, and will only engage as such to speak of the God and Father of our Lord Jesus Christ.

You remark that you have a great dread of offending God by doubting or disbelieving what he wishes us to credit. The feeling of awe and reverence for God cannot possibly be too strong in our hearts, but it must not be allowed to become an emotion of dread, compelling a blind and unreasoning faith in his commands. Far otherwise, my dear friend; we are not only permitted, but commanded to study God's character, as unfolded in the book of nature and of revelation, and unless our belief is founded on an intelligent, rational apprehension of his nature, we cannot possibly be ready, as we are required as Christians to be, ' to give a reason for our faith.' It certainly would be a great sin to disbelieve what we are *assured* God intends us to believe; but that I think is not your case. You doubt whether God does demand belief in a certain thing, and of necessity suspend belief till the doubt is changed into conviction, one way or the other. Such doubts are not in themselves sinful ; on the other hand, all human conviction, even on the most important points, must, in reference to very many things, be attained only after a battle with a whole legion of doubts. 'Is there a God?' is the first question in religion. To ask it implies a doubt if there be a God. Will he forgive sin? implies a similar suspicion that perhaps he will not.

Do not reproach yourself simply because you doubt. God loves to have his character inquired into by his intelligent creatures, and knows that they cannot attain to a knowledge of it till they have disposed of many doubts. The sin is not in doubting, but there will be great sin if we wilfully neglect God's appointed means for removing doubt.

Let us then calmly approach the question of the Trinity, assured that not only shall we not be blamed for searching into it, but that if we come to the inquiry with teachable, childlike natures, and ask God's help, the holy and blessed Father, Son, and Spirit, will reveal themselves unto us, remove our doubts, and guide us into truth.

I rejoice to perceive that much of your difficulty lies in conceiving that it is required of us
as an article of faith to declare that we comprehend or understand how Trinity and Unity co-exist.
Believe me, it is no fond conceit of mine, or any
mistake of yours, that men have exceeded the
Bible in dogmatizing on the Trinity. Nevertheless, the best and wisest have all declared it incomprehensible, and have neither pretended to
understand it themselves, nor asked others to say
they did. Whenever they have attempted to be
' wise above that which is written ' on this subject,
they have only proved their own weakness. You
are perhaps aware that one of the great divisions
in the so-called Christian church, arose out of a
question concerning the nature of the Trinity.
The Greek Church originated in a difference of
opinion between the eastern and western divisions
of the then church. The western or Latin Church
insisted on the creed containing a statement that
' the Holy Ghost proceeds from the Father *and the
Son.*' The eastern or Greek Church refused to in-
troduce the words which I have underlined, and a

schism in consequence occurred. Which of them
was right, if either, is a question which no Christian is called upon to answer. The Church of
England has retained the words of the Latin
creed, but has not defined the sense in which they
are to be understood. I think them quite just
and scriptural, if they signify that the Holy Spirit
never acts independently of the Father and Son;
but if they are intended to teach, as they are in
the mouths of many, the mode or manner in
which the Holy Ghost flows forth from, or eman-
ates from the Godhead, then I humbly decline to
use them, as professing to enter into points on which
Scripture has not enlightened us, and which cannot therefore possibly be articles of Christian faith.
Theology as a science is entitled to discuss such
questions; but we, my friend, who are not dealing
with theology as a science, but reading the Bible
as sinners seeking for salvation, are excused from
their discussion : moreover, be assured of this, that
it is beyond the power of scientific theology to demonstrate the *nature* of the Trinity,—it can only
dimly guess at it.

I will never trouble you with personal views when they are peculiar, at least when I am conscious that they are so. I do not, accordingly, on this occasion, bring before you any views on the Trinity, which are not universally held by other Christians. Now and then differences have arisen among them, like that which divided the Greek and Latin churches, but in general they have abstained from discussion on the *nature* of the Trinity, perceiving that it was beyond human comprehension. Whatever differences may exist among the various parties in the Church of England, they are at one as to the incomprehensibility of the nature of the Trinity. The same remark applies to the Trinitarian dissenters of all classes. It is one of the few points on which Unitarian and Trinitarian would agree, although the latter would of course blame the former for making comprehensibility the test of what should be believed in reference to God. The Roman Catholic and the Protestant would likewise be at one on this matter, at least so far as essentials were concerned, although there might be minor differences

G

on the one side or the other, as to the exact point at which power to comprehend stopped.

The universal consent of Christendom may thus be said to have been given to the doctrine that man must be content to believe, provided sufficient evidence be given, that Trinity and Unity are, in the case of the Godhead, compatible and co-existent, without expecting to understand or comprehend the mode or nature of their co-existence.

I count it, however, so important a point that we should be assured that our God and Father, knowing the limitation of our intellects, has not demanded from us a declaration that we understand what he knows we do not comprehend, that I would refer a little longer to the subject. Till we are satisfied that what we have to do with is the fact, not the nature of it, we waste our time trying to understand the latter, instead of weighing the evidence in proof of the former.

I would refer, in relation to this matter, to the incarnation of our Saviour. The Trinity is not more incomprehensible when taken in connexion with the Divine Unity, than is the union of per-

fect Godhead with perfect sinless manhood in our
Redeemer. How the infinite nature of God should
become united to the finite nature of man, is to
us an utter and inconceivable mystery. Christ
taught his apostles and disciples, and, through
them, all men, that he was God, and proved that
he was by the mighty miracles that he did. That
he was man he also proclaimed, and his enemies
took care that the awful tragedy of the crucifixion
should leave no one in doubt of his humanity.
Belief in our Lord's divinity and humanity was,
not perhaps in so many words, but virtually, required from all who professed faith in him, especially after his resurrection. Yet not once in the
whole New Testament do we find the slightest
explanation offered of the *mode* in which the Divine
and human natures co-existed in the Saviour.
Not Peter their chief, nor John the beloved
apostle, were favoured with insight into the mystery, nor was any lesser apostle or disciple
more favoured. If ever there was an occasion when revelation of the *nature* of his double
life might have been expected from our Sa-

viour, it was when he appeared to his disciples, after his resurrection ; yet he abstained from it, even then, and to the doubting Thomas simply said, 'Stretch forth thine hand.' 'Believe that I am God-man ; *how*, concerns thee not, and is beyond thy comprehension.' So fully does this avoidance of even the slightest appearance of unfolding the mystery of Christ's nature appear in Scripture, that one of the inspired writers states as a thing most manifest, unquestionable, and to be accepted as true by every Christian, 'Great is the mystery of godliness, God manifest in the flesh.'

If our Saviour, however, did not reveal the nature of his co-existent divinity and humanity, as little did he demand from any one, as an article of faith, or requisite to salvation, profession of comprehension of it. 'Thy faith,' said he to many a sinner, 'hath saved thee; go in peace.' The faith was simply in his being the Son of God, at the same time that he was perceived to be the Son of man. No one of those whose cases are recorded in the Gospels refers to the mystery of his Divine-human nature as a thing he comprehended. In like manner, when the jailer at Philippi asked, 'What shall I do to be saved?' the answer was, 'Believe on the Lord Jesus Christ, and thou shalt be saved.' Believe that the Man Christ Jesus was also the Lord Jesus, or Christ and God, and salvation is thine.

I observe, in passing, that it is not my purpose, in the last few sentences, to imply that mere belief in Christ's divinity is enough to secure salvation. It was, of course, essential to this that they should accept Christ as a Mediator and a Redeemer, as well as regard him as God. Into this I do not for the present enter. What I am earnestly anxious to impress upon you is, that it forms an essential part of the scheme of revelation, to require our assent to mysteries, and that, therefore, instead of reproaching yourself for not understanding the nature of the Trinity, you should simply concern yourself with the question, Is there evidence of the unity and trinity of God? If there be, we need no more suspend belief in it till we understand it, which we never shall, than we need decline to believe in Christ's humanity and divinity, because the mode of their conjunction is to us incomprehensible. For that matter, the mode of union of our minds and bodies is to us an utter mystery; yet we do not hold ourselves excused from believing in both on that account.

This, then, premised, I suppose I need not enter into any lengthened exposition of the *unity* of the Godhead. It is not in reference to it that the difficulty is mainly felt. The Bible so unmistakably teaches that God is *one*, that no reader of it can doubt his unity. One passage may suffice : 'The Lord our God is one Lord.'

Then as to the Trinity. The two passages containing the formula of baptism and the apostolical benediction, are the texts which, I believe, mention together, as equal and divine, the Father, Son, and Spirit. But we must not expect to find the Trinity systematically expounded in single texts, as it is expressed in our Church creeds and confessions of faith. A friend of mine,—a most devoted, earnest, and pious minister, and, moreover, of all the intellectual men I count among my friends, the man of greatest grasp and intellectual capacity, according to my humble judgment,—said to me one day, whilst we were talking together of the Trinity, in which he is a most profound believer, 'I do not think the Trinity is revealed in Scripture *more* than could possibly be helped.' In other words, he thought that God's nature was taught us in the Bible solely to the extent that was necessary for enabling us to know it, so that the weakest sane intellect should find nothing to stumble at when seeking to discover how forgiveness of sin and peace with God might be attained. It—*i.e.*, the Bible—was intended not only for the subtle spirits and acute intellects of the world, but likewise for the 'not many wise' who have souls to save, as well as the greatly gifted ; and whilst its depths cannot be reached by the plummet of the loftiest human or angelic intellect, its essential truths can be apprehended by those of capacity the most limited.

Hence, there is no such perplexing thing as an Athanasian or even Apostles' Creed in the New

Testament. These are excellent, admirable things in their way, for those who have intellect to reach to their appreciation; but I doubt not that in heaven, among those last in this world, but first in that to come, there are many spirits of just men made perfect to whom these words were hopeless and unthought-of incomprehensibilities when on earth.

I have made a long digression on this matter, but, I trust, not an unnecessary one, though I have to crave your indulgence for a letter written at irregular, broken intervals. What I would now add is this: without looking in the New Testament for demonstrations of the Trinity, and without expecting such, let us inquire whether there is evidence that the Father is God. You are persuaded already, I think, that he is. Secondly, you are, I think, satisfied that the Son is God. Thirdly, you do not doubt the *personality* of the Spirit,—a great matter, my friend; for if we perceive that the New Testament plainly proclaims of the Holy Spirit, not that *it*, but that *he* is, we shall very soon come to the conclusion that his attributes, his office, and his operations, as referred to, even incidentally in Scripture, are such as belong to and can be discharged by none but God. I shall presently quote some texts in support of this position; but I am anxious to pave the way for their reception. Suppose, then, that you are satisfied that unity is attributed in the Scriptures to God; secondly, that Father, Son, and Spirit have both divinity ascribed to them, and personality or individuality, so that, in some sense *not* explained by the Bible, to us quite mysterious, there is, if I may use the phrase, a co-existent threeness and oneness attributed to God. Suppose also that you are convinced that we are not asked to declare that we understand this three-oneness, but are simply desired to profit by it; then I put the question, Ought we to stumble at the mystery of the Trinity, simply because it is mysterious? Surely not, if we believe in God at all.

I select, then, after stating this, a few texts in reference to the Holy Spirit. In the fourteenth and two succeeding chapters of St. John's Gospel, we have a record of that remarkable conversation which Christ held with his disciples concerning the Holy Spirit. In the sixteenth chapter it is said of the latter, 'When he is come, he will reprove the world of sin, of righteousness, and of judgment;' and 'when the Spirit of truth is come, he will guide you into *all* truth,' is attributed to the Spirit ; in other words, infinite knowledge or omniscience is ascribed to the Holy Ghost. This implies divinity, for God only is omniscient. In Acts xiii. 2-4 : 'As they ministered to the Lord, and fasted, the Holy Spirit said, Separate ME Barnabas and Saul for the work whereunto *I have called them.*' In this passage the Spirit asserts a power to set apart whom he pleases, to whatever work he wills to call him. It is further mentioned that Saul and Barnabas, 'being sent forth *by the Holy Spirit,* departed.' Here God's creatures are called, commanded, and sent forth, by one who must either be the rival, or the equal of God in power to control them. I think here again we have a divine prerogative attributed to the Spirit. In Acts xv. and xvi. these

expressions occur : ' It seemed good to the Holy
Ghost ;' certain parties were ' forbidden of the
Holy Ghost ;' ' the Spirit suffered them not.'
In these three passages we have the Spirit acting
as one who had no superior, in so far as right to
command men was concerned. ' All these work-
eth that one and the self-same Spirit, dividing to
every man severally *as he will*' (1 Cor. xii. 11).
Here, surely, sovereignty and supremacy of will
are ascribed to the Holy Ghost, and in a way
so unlimited as to imply at once possession to
the fullest, of the highest attribute of the Godhead, if I may so speak, viz., a will which none
other can control, and before which all must
bend.   In Acts v. 3, 4, Peter asks Ananias why
he had been induced ' to lie to the Holy Ghost,'
and afterwards adds, ' Thou hast not lied unto
men, but unto God.'   Here the apostle seems
plainly to affirm that to lie to the Holy Ghost
and to God are the same thing.   In 1 Cor. iii.
16, occur the words, ' Know ye not that ye are
the temple of God, and that the Spirit of God
dwelleth in you?'   Again, in chapter vi. 19,

'What ! know ye not that your body is the temple of the Holy Ghost, which ye have of God ?' 'And what agreement hath the temple of God with idols ? for ye are the temple of the living God ; as God hath said, I will dwell in them, and walk in them' (2 Cor. vi. 16). Here the Christian is spoken of as the temple of the Holy Ghost *or* of God, the phrases plainly being synonymous, interchangeable, and of equal value. Of the following very striking passage, I shall quote only the last few words for brevity's sake : —'The Spirit searcheth *all* things, yea, the deep things of God. . . . The things of God knoweth no man (or no one), but the Spirit of God' (1 Cor. ii. 9-11). Who, my friend, can this omniscient *Person* be, cognisant of all that God knows, partaker (if the word be admissible) and possessor of his deepest thoughts ? Who can he be but God ? In that splendid poem, that grand hymn of praise, the 139th Psalm, the question is asked, 'Whither shall I (the psalmist, or any one) flee from *thy Spirit ?*' Here omnipresence and omniscience are directly and unreservedly, fully and not by implication, attributed and imputed to the Spirit, as I think you will not doubt, if you read the whole Psalm. Prescience or foreknowledge is in like manner declared to be a quality of the Spirit. St. Peter declares that 'holy men of God (the prophets) were moved *by the Holy Ghost*' (2 Pet. i. 20). St. Paul ascribes eternal existence to the Spirit : ' How much more shall the blood of Christ, who through *the Eternal Spirit* offered himself' (Heb. ix. 14).

After these passages (and there are many similar) are read singly first, and then together, let the apostolical benediction and the baptismal formula be considered as gathering them into one, and is it possible to doubt that the Bible teaches that the Holy Spirit is first a person ; secondly, a divine person ; thirdly, God? I think no Socinian pleader, who accepts the Scriptures as inspired, authentic, and genuine, can defend himself against the force of these remarkable affirmations of the Bible.

January 24th, 1848.

THE enclosed[1] has already reached to a length so unreasonable, that I think it best to despatch it, imperfect as it is, especially as I have no prospect of being able to resume it for a day or two. I will, however, without troubling you to answer it, send a further statement shortly.

Meanwhile, I would only add one word on what I had hoped to reach the discussion of, without covering so much paper, viz., How is the consciousness of guilt and remorse at past mis-spent time to be appeased? In one way only, my friend, —by prayer to God for forgiveness. This may seem a mere truism, but I am sure we all err in looking into our hearts in hope to find some worth, some holiness, some source of peace and joy there. This is our great and grievous mistake; never shall we find in ourselves anything but sin, disaffection to God, and disobedience to his law. Do not wait till you find greater love in your heart and mind for God. It was while we were yet in our sins that Christ died for us; it is as sinners,

---

[1] This is a postscript to the preceding letter.

not as the righteous, that he will mediate and intercede for us. Earnest prayer is the only means whereby we can obtain an interest in Christ's blood, the help of the Holy Spirit, and the forgiveness of the Father. We are to go with all our sins, our remorses, our agonies of conscience, our sense of guilt and feeling of deserved punishment, to the throne of God's grace to beseech for mercy. God's ear is ever open, and he is more ready to give than we to ask, more willing to answer than we to request. Take him, my dear friend, *at his word:* believe that God 'is a rewarder of those that diligently seek him,' and seek till you find him. Find him you will, if you but search. It is his Holy Spirit that is striving with yours, for though it is impossible, and would be unwise to try to distinguish between the teachings of our consciences and the warnings of the Spirit, yet of this we need have no doubt, that the Holy Spirit is the author of that deep sense of demerit which agonizes you. You have cause to thank God for this: it is the beginning of peace with him.

My advice, as one who have known the united
tortures you describe, is for the present couched
in the two words,—the Bible and prayer. 'Ask,
and you *shall* receive,' are Christ's own words,
and will be answered to you, as they have been
to thousands, if you will but pray and watch,
and watch and pray. The post waits. I will write
very soon.

May 14th, 1848.

I would have written to you long before this,
had I not been poorly, and in particular so plagued
with rheumatism in my arm that it was painful to
write, and I was compelled to dictate to my sister.

It rejoiced me to learn from your last letter
that G. was better, and I encourage the hope
that he, too, will, through God's blessing, find this
genial weather help him rapidly on towards entire
recovery.

I will not attempt to take up our correspondence at the point where it dropped, but begin,
as it were, anew: although, in truth, our religious
wants being ever the same, and our difficulties

and perplexities substantially identical from season
to season, there cannot be other than compara-
tively small differences between the objects of
Christian interest at one time and at another. I
do not fear, therefore, that I can much err in
selecting any topic that bears upon our relation to
God. Nor can I but deeply sympathize with so
great a loss as that which you deplore, viz., the
absence of a Christian circle, in which you could
profit by the interchange of opinion, and the solution of doubts, which others who had got beyond
them, might be able to solve for you ; and where—
beside those whom natural gift and God's calling,
and the experience of years of holy living, and
his grace largely granted, had peculiarly qualified
to stretch a helping hand to young and less advanced brethren—you might be encouraged to run
boldly, and see stumblingblocks removed, which at
one time threatened to make so much as walking
impossible. For this great want, however, a remedy
is to be found. God will, we may be sure, keep
from us no good thing we need. Religious friends
and suitable counsellors will not be withheld from

us ; but whilst we pray for such, we must be careful to see that we are not overlooking opportunities of Christian intercourse which are within our reach, and must use a considerate discretion in selecting acquaintances and friends. This is a point on which none of us are free. We must hold intercourse with many who are not the 'excellent of the earth.' We should act very wrongfully, if we abruptly flung away the long-enduring friendship of some who may nevertheless come far short of what our consciences and our Bibles tell us our bosom friends should be. No one, moreover, can know the peculiarities of another's position in this respect, or be in a condition to offer more than limited advice. I have myself, however, been so great a sufferer from neglect of Christian prudence in this respect, and so great a gainer from the cultivation of the friendship of devout men and women, and I feel so strong a temptation to forget what experience satisfies me is wisdom in this matter, that I am not afraid to offend you, by including you in the accusation I prefer against myself.

The sympathy I feel with Art, Literature, and Science, makes me tolerant of much that I cannot approve of in those who are great in these departments; and a similar relish for what is estimable in lesser things, leads me to excuse what I grieve to witness. Your wide sympathies, I think, must lead you also to be charitable in weighing the faults of the gifted and the warm-hearted. We require, however, to guard very sedulously, lest our Catholicism become Latitudinarianism. A large acquaintance on the part of one with *many* morally below him, but intellectually his equals or superiors, is much more likely to end in their dragging him down to their level than in his lifting them to his.

I am afraid you will think that I am preaching to you a dry sermon, but I am about to cut it short by this remark. Let us at least be wary in choosing *new* friends. When God sends to us (as he has done to you and me) much affliction, he says, as it were, 'Set your house in order.' He lays us aside from active work, or sends us into retirement, and there in mercy provides us with leisure, we never could, or thought we never could,

procure, and bids us, with eyes opened to the un-
abidingness of earthly happiness, review the past
and consider the future. We cannot look into our
hearts, and out into the world, in the spirit which
God desires us to maintain, without feeling that
if the future is to be less barren and unfruitful
than the past, it must be by our obeying God
better. Now, obedience to his law implies but two
things, viz., entire love of him, and of his children.
So much is this insisted on in the Bible, that the existence of the one love is tested by the existence of
the other; and the presence of both in our hearts
is the proof that we are God's people. Thus, the
apostle John says, 'We know that we have passed
from death unto life, because we love the brethren'
(1 John iii. 14); and again, the other side of the
question, 'By this we know that we love the children of God, when we love God, and keep his commandments' (1 John v. 2). Surely, then, to love,
and to prefer the society of the children of God, is
not merely a plain, but an indispensable duty, and
if God is pleased to deny us the opportunity of
much Christian intercourse, he is only the more

calling on us, to avoid, at least, mingling with the unchristian world.

I have dilated on this point far longer than I intended to have done. It was on another thing I purposed to dwell. The Christian, however cut off from human Christian friendships, is nevertheless the very opposite of friendless. Has he not in Christ Jesus one who, we are told, is 'a friend that sticketh closer than a brother:' who is 'our elder brother,' the 'first-born among many brethren,' 'not ashamed to call us brethren.' His people are spoken of, not merely as '*heirs*,' but as '*fellow*-heirs' with him of glory. The Unitarian looks on these and similar passages as testimonies only to the humanity of Christ. Irreligious men pronounce the notion that God stands in the relation of a friend or brother to man his creature, as incredible and perhaps ridiculous folly. Nevertheless, the Bible most explicitly assures us of the fact, and that not obscurely or in passages of doubtful meaning, but in the plainest announcements, of which it is full.

The Unitarian view cannot profit us, for, what

though Christ had a friendly feeling towards us, it will avail us nothing on this earth, if he be but a man not existent upon it; not omniscient, so that he should know what our wants are, or hear our prayers; not omnipresent, so that he could be at the same time with all his suffering people; nor omnipotent, so that he could save to the uttermost.'

Many worthy Trinitarians also, for fear of seeming to sanction Socinian doctrine, put Christ's human nature in the background, in a way he did not himself, and his disciples do not, and hide from us one of the sources of our Saviour's love and sympathy for his brethren. The apostles had no fear of weakening the stability of the doctrine that Christ was God, by teaching that he was man. In their writings we find both truths urged, and urged together, as causes and proofs of the peculiar relation in which the Lord Jesus Christ stands to his people. I would specially direct your attention to the Epistle to the Hebrews, as enforcing in its practical bearings the double truth. In the first chapter, Christ's equality with God the Father, and his superiority to angels, *i.e.*, the mightiest

creatures, is insisted on, as if it were the only
truth the apostle had to teach. In the second
chapter, nevertheless, the humanity of our Saviour,
and his inferiority as man to the angels, is quite
as fully dwelt on. The apostle had no hesitation
as to declaring the *whole* counsel of God—not only
no fear that he would disturb the minds of his
readers by teaching an apparently contradictory
doctrine, but a certainty that all who were spiritually enlightened would find the double truth rich
in divinely purposed fulness of consolation and
promise, which half of that truth could not possibly
supply. Because Christ is God, he can say, ' I will
never leave thee, nor forsake thee.' ' Lo ! I am
with you alway.' ' Where two or three are gathered
together in my name, there am I in the midst of
you to bless you.' Because he was ' a man of
sorrows, and acquainted with grief,' it can be said
of him, ' In all their afflictions he was afflicted ;'
' himself took our infirmities, and bare our sick-
nesses ;' ' he was in all points tempted like as we are,
yet without sin.' And because he was both God
and (sinless) man, it can be proclaimed, ' For in

that he 'himself hath suffered, being tempted, he is able to succour them that are tempted;' and again, 'We have not a high priest which cannot be touched with the feeling of our infirmities. . . . . Let us therefore come boldly unto the throne of grace, that we may obtain mercy, and find grace to help in time of need.' What a practical doctrine the truth of Christ's associated divinity and humanity thus becomes : something very unlike what it appears in polemical treatises, and systems of scientific theology. Who can, if willing, be such a friend to us, as Christ can be? His divine omniscience secures his knowledge of our state; his ubiquity makes him 'near to each one of us.' His omnipotence invests him with infinite power to succour us. Then he looks not at us in our sorrows only with the awful eye of the all-knowing God, but with the sympathizing gaze of the once suffering, sinless man. And of his willingness to help we are as certain as of his power. He utters from heaven what he spoke on earth, 'Come unto me, all ye that labour and are heavy laden, and I will give you rest.'

May we both, my dear friend, be admitted to fellow-heirship with him, and be able, each of us, with the once doubting, but then believing, Thomas to say, 'My Lord and my God!'

June 4th, 1848.

DEAR MRS. Y.,—A plaguy rheumatism that troubles my right and *writ*-ing arm prevented my taking up the pen last Sabbath; but this evening I resume it, trusting to your telling me when I tire you.

There is a very remarkable verse, viz., the 17th in the seventh chapter of St. John's Gospel, which at first appears startling, but afterwards appears most encouraging. It is this, 'If any man will do God's will, he shall know of the doctrine whether it be of God.' We are to begin, not with demonstration of *all* God's claims to our obedience being supplied to us, and then to be required to render him service. But knowledge is to come after, and be the recompense of obedience. It certainly is not the aim of the verse to teach, that one absolutely ignorant of God's nature is to obey him. Christ spoke the words to the Jews who knew much concerning God; had he been addressing heathens, he would have taught them concerning the Father, before he required their obedience to him. What was enforced on the Jews and on us is, I think, that as soon as we are furnished with grounds sufficient for entitling God to claim our services, we are not to postpone rendering these till we comprehend fully all his relations, but are at once to conform ourselves to his will so far as we know it. The doing of God's will at so early a stage of our knowledge of him, instead of leading us to an imperfect acquaintance with his character, or inducing a limited perception of his nature, will, our Saviour's words assure us, lead us into such a knowledge of the doctrine, *i.e.*, the whole scheme of God's dealing with men, as in no other way could we attain.

A little thought will, I think, satisfy us that the method of procedure here pointed out, is a most natural one, which at once commends itself to us, as alike natural and wise, indeed the best, the only possible plan. Is it not the way in which every child reaches to knowledge of its earthly father? How mysterious must the relationship to its parents be for years to every child! Long after cravings for this knowledge have arisen, it could not, owing to their dimness, express them in words; and after it is mature enough to be able to shape its difficulties into articulate questions, it could not, by any possibility, understand the answers its parents should give. The latter, however desirous, can by no means accommodate the matter to the child's limited capacity. The endeavour to explain one difficulty, only ends in filling the infant's mind with a thousand new difficulties; he is harmed, not profited, by an answer having been rendered to him. The wise parent says, ' When you are a little older, I will tell you,' and the child who does his father's will, by and by reaps the fruit of his obedience.

No parent counts his child excused from obedience because he does not fully apprehend his father's relation to him. The child knows *enough*. The father counts upon the instinctive love which he knows God has implanted in the child's heart. He can appeal to the kindness he has shown his offspring, the sacrifices he has made for it, the toils he has endured for it, and can say, I have given you sufficient and ample grounds for trusting me, trust me then, and by and by you shall be furnished with much fuller proofs of the reasonableness of my claims upon you.

And how much more does this hold with our God and Father, whose love and wisdom have not, like those exhibited by earthly parents, been imperfectly shown forth, but have been manifested with infinite fulness and freeness?

The sum of all this, my dear friend, is, that in seeking to know God, we are for a time to set aside the notion of making progress in *knowledge,* and to think only of making progress in *obedience;* but behold, before we have got far on with the latter, we find that the former, which we thought was left behind, has been keeping pace side by side with the obedience which we thought had no connexion with it.

Nor is there anything mystical in all this. The

two great requirements of our Father in heaven are, 'Love God, love man.' The practical directions are likewise two, 'Search the Scriptures, for they are they that testify of me,' and 'Pray without ceasing.' The searching of the Scriptures is to be carried on in the spirit of discovering God's will, not of stumbling at the difficulties. The prayer is to be for the Spirit's help to understand what He, the author of the book, intended by each passage. The searching and the prayer are to go on together. David prayed that God would 'teach him wondrous things out of his law ;' and Christ, when delivering his farewell address to his disciples, told them that 'the Spirit of truth' would 'guide them into all truth.' Our Saviour adds, 'He shall not speak of himself, . . . he shall glorify me ;' and in another place, ' He shall testify of me.' Now, the Spirit of truth is not only sent by the Son, but he proceedeth from the Father also ; he is the divine interpreter of God's will. He is God, revealing God to us.

Now, which is the more hopeful plan, to gaze with the dim eye of human intellect on the mys-

teries of revelation, like men poring for hours over
undecipherable hieroglyphics, or to take God at
his word, to believe the Father and the Son, as we
credit men who never deceived us, when those
divine persons assure us that God loves to hear
and to answer prayer? Surely it were better, in
obedience to God's will, to ask for his Spirit, and
the granting of this request could not in the nature
of things but immensely extend our knowledge.
For who, to take that great mystery of the Trinity,
shall enlighten us as the divine Spirit who is of it,
and who never comes without the consent and high
approbation of the Father and the Son?

I believe there is no solution for the mystery of
that doctrine, but that of communion with the
Trinity. The Christian who can sincerely call
God Father, not as pretending to exhibit a perfect
child-like obedience to him,—for 'if we say we have
no sin, we deceive ourselves, and the truth is not
in us,'—but as seeking in honest sincerity not to
act as a mere subject acknowledging him with
a certain easy loyalty as a king, or as a servant
obeying a master, or a slave fearing a tyrant; but

as a son lifting up his face freely before a father whom he reverences and adores, and to satisfy the just wishes of whom is the great business of his life. The man who lives in the Spirit, and who adds to it the deepest love for Christ, and most anxious desire to imitate his example, and to devote himself to his service ; who labours in his cause, and who is conscious of a hatred of sin and a disrelish for follies he once loved, with a long-ing for increasing holiness and fof conformity to God, such as the Bible declares the Holy Spirit only produces in any human breast ;—he who is thus bound by invisible ties to the forgiving Father, the atoning Son, and the sanctifying Spirit, can well afford to adjourn, till he reaches heaven, the revelation of the mysteries of their oneness and threeness. His great concern is to profit by his union to them.

I'fancy you saying when you read this, ' So I am to become a perfect Christian, and then I shall understand the Trinity !' Nay, my dear friend, there is no perfect Christian on earth. The Christian life is a *life*, beginning with a (new) birth, and growing up through living stages till death transplants the so-far mature Christian to heaven, but only to a higher life, which will never cease to grow and expand; else why an eternity for it? There was not one even of the apostles that did not groan being burdened with sin, all his days. The greater our holiness, the greater our sensitiveness to sin. Be not disheartened if you are behind others, provided only you are going on. To be able to say, 'Lord, I believe, help mine unbelief,' should be cause of thankfulness. To lament our sin is a proof that God's Spirit has not left us as hopeless.

There is a remarkable promise in the Bible, 'Unto him that hath shall be given.' Learn a little of God's will, and obey it, and to you rather than to another, he will reveal himself more fully.

Forgive the haste of this letter, and believe me,

Your attached friend.

July 9th, 1848.

DEAR MRS. Y.,—I should have written to you long ago, had I not been complaining much as you are yourself. For the last two months, I have had a constant sense of 'unwellness,' a disrelish of all work, and reluctance to do anything I could excuse myself from doing. I mention this simply to excuse myself for not writing, not to make complaint to you who have illness and sorrow enough to vex you.

Looking at most things from the same point of view as you are doing, especially in so far as personal health is concerned, I fall back more and more on prayer, as an amazing instrument put into our hands, as it were, by God, to bring down blessings upon us. There is something very wonderful in the way in which, all throughout the Bible, prayer is referred to. That we should be permitted to intrude on the all-perfect One with our little requests seems at first not credible. Is the ruler of the universe to be interrupted every moment by the beseechings of the children of

I

men? Is he to turn aside, now to this one, now to that, and dispose of graciously or ungraciously —(answer in some way) every petition? It has seemed to many, unworthy of God so to employ himself, and at variance with the observed uniformity of natural laws, to expect an answer to prayer; and those who speak thus regard themselves as honouring God more than the Christian does, by relieving the Almighty of all concern in the entreaties of his creatures.

If we truly, however, and honestly believe God to be infinite in all his attributes, and literally interpret the title Almighty, then we cannot for a moment imagine that the unintermitting prayers of a few millions of men can overtask Omnipotence. It is a low, not a lofty, or honouring estimate of God, which conceives that he can in the least be burdened by listening to the requests of his creatures. Those who speak as if he could, impeach his omnipotence, and deny his infinity, without which he would cease to be God. He may decline to listen to prayer, but assuredly not because he is inadequate to the task of attending to it.

There is nothing then in the nature of God, opposed to prayer. Nor is there anything in the regularity of natural laws; for if it be true that God is a prayer-hearing and answering God, then the laws he has imposed on nature, are certain to have been framed in harmony with prayer, so as to admit of its being offered up without contradicting them. Thousands of earnest prayers have been offered to God, that he would keep Great Britain in peace and prosperity. Disbelievers in the efficacy of prayer will impute her happiness to her Government, Parliament, soil; to the physical and intellectual character of her people, etc. etc.; but who can tell to what extent these secondary causes have been shaped to good, and moulded by God in consequence of prayer, not as an unexpected thing inducing the Almighty to change his plans, but as an anticipated and pre-ordained element, taking its appointed place in determining events? God gives us a national character : true! but he also puts it into our hearts to pray to him. The one does not contradict the other. Each plays its part in working out the purposes of God, and each is equally natural.

It is not in the power of any man to disprove the efficacy of prayer, for men have been praying since the world began, and what influence their prayers have had on its destinies no one can tell. He may assume that they have had no influence, but he cannot prove this.

I think it a great matter to perceive this, and to be certain that no one can prove that prayer is folly. That it is the highest wisdom, is the declaration of Revelation, and the book of nature not only does not utter a syllable in contradiction of this, but in truth confirms it. No nation has been found in which men did not pray. They have widely differed in the nature of their estimate of the character of the being or beings to whom they prayed, and as to the objects of their prayers. Yet, after all, there has been an amazing unanimity. All have believed that there was a hearer of prayer : all have deprecated wrath; entreated that punishment might be stayed; and besought good gifts.

A universal and ineradicable instinct makes man an offerer of prayer. It is strange, indeed, to observe how the very oaths and curses of those who mock God are acknowledgments of his existence and power, and are actual prayers. He who uses the word 'damn' is, unconsciously it may be, implying his belief that there is one who does 'condemn;' and petitioning him to put in force his awful power. Nor are such prayers unanswered.

Nature then bids us pray, without fearing to clash with other natural things. God permits, encourages, and commands prayer. He not only says, you *may* pray, but you may pray imploringly, beseechingly, importunately; he further adds, you *must* pray, if you would prove yourselves my children.

The authorizing of even' importunate prayer is a remarkable feature of the Bible. Abraham is permitted when pleading for Sodom, to expostulate, as it were, with God (Genesis xviii.) Jacob *wrestles* for a blessing till he receives it (Genesis xxxii. 25). Our Saviour is spoken of, in Hebrews (v. 7), as having, when a suffering man, been heard 'when he had offered up prayers and supplications with strong crying and tears.' This was his example. His precept was in conformity with it, and is strikingly enforced in two of the parables. The one is that of the party begging from his neighbour the loan of bread, and receiving it in the middle of the night, *' because of his importunity'* (Luke xi. 5-8). The other parable is that of the widow and the unjust judge, where she gained her end, as the result of 'her *continual coming'* (Luke xviii. 5). When the whole Bible so plainly exhorts us to frequent, earnest, importunate, wrestling, and agonistic prayer, well may the apostle James say, 'Ye have not, because ye ye ask not' (iv. 2).

But then comes the question, How shall we pray? Will any kind 'of importunity, or clamorous, inconsiderate besieging of God's throne be acceptable to him? Nay, far from it. The same apostle James also says, 'Ye ask, and receive not, because ye ask amiss' (iv. 3).

And this brings us back to the Trinity, and the practical value of clear views on it becomes apparent. God is the great Judge, administering his own righteous laws. He at once ordains, administers, and executes the laws of his kingdom. To him, the Father, we address ourselves in prayer, and he has appointed the mode in which he is to be approached and addressed. Our earthly sovereigns do not permit their subjects to petition them in any way they think proper, but refer them to certain fixed channels and appointed officials, through whom alone requests can be received. In our courts of justice, it is imperative that petitions for the interference of the judge shall be drawn up in certain prescribed forms, otherwise they are refused consideration. Nor is any one free to plead in court, but only authorized barristers or advocates, who alone are permitted to urge the petitioner's claims and use intercession.

So it is—though the comparison is altogether insufficient—in the court of heaven; court alike of royalty and of justice. The suitor in the Queen's Bench requires both the attorney to prepare the pleading, and the barrister to urge its justice, otherwise the judge turns a deaf ear.

And how is it at the throne of grace, and before the great Judge? '*We* know not what we should pray for as we ought,' says the apostle Paul; but he adds, 'the Spirit also helpeth our infirmities.' The whole eighth chapter of the Romans, in which the words I have quoted occur, is full of the doctrine, as the whole Bible is, that one of the offices of the Holy Spirit is to teach us how to pray, to frame our petitions for us, so that they shall be acceptable to God; to enable us to draw up our pleadings in the 'Spirit of grace and supplication'—the only language permitted at the bar of God.

The attorney's pleading does not go directly to the judge. It stops with the barrister, or, as he is called in *this* country, the advocate, who lays its substance before the court. And what saith the Scriptures? 'If any man sin, we have an *Advocate* with the Father, Jesus Christ the righteous' (1 John ii. 1). The blessed Saviour, who ever liveth to make intercession for us, receives gladly every petition which has the mark of the Spirit upon it, and presents it to the Father, by whom, be sure, it is answered in grace and love, though not, it may be, as the petitioner expected. There is no division in their holy counsels. What the Spirit sanctions, the Son approves, and the Father ratifies. Blessed and consoling thought! 'This is the confidence that we have in him' (the Son of God), says with peaceful assurance the apostle John, 'that, if we ask anything according to his will, he heareth us. And if we know that he hear us, whatsoever we ask, we know that we have the petitions that we desired of him' (1 John v. 14, 15). The Spirit enables us to 'ask according to the Son's will,' and with the Son the Father is ever well pleased.

My dear friend, when one has got to understand and to believe this, and to use prayer with the conviction that the aid of each Person of the Godhead is essential to its acceptability as Christian prayer, the Trinity ceases to be an object of merely intellectual contemplation, or a stumblingblock to the reason; and the grateful and adoring heart claims it as the most precious and certain of blessed realities.

May it be given to us, and to all we love, to have the sanctifying help of the Holy Spirit, and the redeeming love of the blessed Son, and the benignant forgiveness of our heavenly Father !

Oct. 14th, 1850.

DEAR MRS. Y., — I have found it more diffi-cult than I expected to find suitable works to send you on the peculiarities of Presbyterianism. They are all too long, formal, and systematic, and would take weeks to read. I shall forward, by railway, the smallest and most manageable among them ; and meanwhile, I shall try in this letter to convey to you, in a few words, as clear an account as I can of the difference between Presbyterianism and the system under which you have been brought up [Episcopacy]. It will come out more clearly if I begin by noticing that there are three great religious associations, variously divided in this country. They name themselves churches, and each claims to be the purest and truest representative and copy of what the Church of Christ was in the days of our Saviour, both as respects method of church government and discipline, and creed or doctrine. The one of these associations is Episcopal, the second Presbyterian, the third Congregational. These names have reference to the method of church government, not to the peculiar doctrines; so that, for example, the Roman Catholics, as well as the Church of England, are episcopal, agreeing to a very great extent in mode of government, but differing in doctrine; and the Unitarians are some of them Congregational, others Presbyterian, although the immense majority, both of Congregationalists and Presbyterians, are most decided Trinitarians. Of the Congregationalists I shall say very little: they are the body to which I myself belong, and for that reason I will leave them very much alone. A reference, however, to their general polity will make the peculiarities of the other bodies more apparent. In a word, then, the Episcopalian form of church government may be said to be monarchical; that of the Presbyterians, representative or republican; that of the Congrega-

tionalists, purely democratic.   In the Church of
England, for example, there is a bishop, whose
rule and authority are like those of a prince
over the priests, deacons, and laymen of his diocese.   He only can ordain priests and deacons.
He only can confirm laymen.   He has authority
over the clergy, who must submit to his guidance,
and must be ruled within certain limits by his de-
cisions; and these apply to a particular large
section of the country, or of one of its colonial
possessions, over the whole of which he has
spiritual jurisdiction.   There are thus in the
Church of England four constituent parts — the
laity, the deacons (who cannot administer all the
sacraments, or perform all the services of the
Church), the priests or fully-ordained clergymen,
and the bishop.   If we look now at Congregationalism, we shall find the opposite extreme.
Instead of three grades of clergy or ministers,
there is but one, and each congregation rules itself without any control or interference from
other congregations or other ministers than its
own.   I beg your attention to this peculiarity, as

it will make Presbyterianism clearer. In the church, then, for example, of which I am a member, there are but two constituent parts, the minister and the people. The minister is ordained by other ministers, but is chosen by his flock; and between him and them, or over them, there is no interfering or controlling power. Every member of the church has a voice and vote in all the proceedings of the congregation, and all are equal except the minister, who is superior. There are deacons in our churches, but their official duties correspond generally to those of your churchwardens, and they have no spiritual authority. They are chosen by the members of the whole church, and are set apart by the minister.

Presbyterianism is intermediate between Episcopalianism and Congregationalism. In Congregationalism the people are supreme; in Presbyterianism the power is divided between both; in it all ministers are of equal rank, there being no distinction as of deacon, priest, and bishop in the Episcopal church. The congregation are not all equal, nor has each member of it a voice in the proceedings of their churches. As in Parliament the whole nation is in the House of Commons represented by delegates who are chosen by the people, who do not themselves directly speak or vote in the assemblies of the nation,—so, in the Presbyterian body, the congregation is represented by a small number of persons selected from it, who are called elders. They have a spiritual rank. Along with the minister they constitute a committee, or *Session* as it is called, who conduct the affairs of the church. They, for example, examine applicants for admission to the church, decide on their being made members or not, visit the sick and the poor of the congregation, pray and read the Scriptures with those of the church who may desire or require their presence, and at the communion assist the minister in the distribution of the bread and wine, which are offered to communicants in a different way in the Congregational and Presbyterian from that of the Episcopal churches. The elders of the Presbyterian churches thus discharge religious offices. They do not preach, however, or administer baptism, or ever take the place of the minister at the communion. Only those who are ordained ministers discharge those duties. A single Presbyterian church (by which I here mean a congregation of professed Christians uniting in a particular building, and all members, not mere hearers) has thus a minister, a session or committee of elders, and a body of members. The last-named act—at least in the Established Church of Scotland—through the session, and have no direct voice in the majority of proceedings, except in the election of ministers, where the members of the congregation are allowed more directly to interfere. A Presbyterian congregation, however, does not stand alone, like a congregational one, ruling itself. All the congregations of one district are represented by what is called its Presbytery. This corresponds so far, if I mistake not, to the office of the archdeacon in the English Church, who comes between the bishop and the parish clergy. In this presbytery all the ministers of the district meet together at stated times, and along with them more or fewer of the elders of those

churches. They have authority over the several
churches in the district. No minister can be appointed to a particular congregation without their
consent and approval, and appeals may be made
to the presbytery by even the smallest minority in
a congregation, who are not satisfied with the proceedings of their minister and session. Further,
all the presbyteries of a large district of country
meet at intervals and constitute a Synod. Thus
there may be five, six, or seven presbyteries in a
county, which meeting together form the Synod
of that county. It corresponds so far to your
bishop ruling over a diocese, including various
archdeaconries, which in their turn include various
parishes. The synod is a court of appeal from
the presbyteries. A party, for example, dissatisfied
with the decision of the presbytery of which the
church of which he is a member forms a part, may
appeal to the synod of his district, and have the
whole matter reconsidered. Finally, once a year
all the synods, or representatives from them all,
i.e., ministers and elders from every presbytery,
meet together in Edinburgh, and form the General

Assembly of the Church. This is the final court of appeal, to which matters may be referred from the synod, and there they are finally disposed of. Further, this General Assembly legislates on all matters affecting the church as a whole. The duties of this body correspond so far to those of an archbishop, but its powers are much greater.

Such then is a brief outline of Presbyterianism. It looks complex on paper, but remember it is really less complex than Episcopalianism, and works better than the latter does, at least at present, for all parties in England seem to wish a Convocation, which Government forbids to them, but sanctions in the General Assembly to the Church of Scotland, of which it is the annual convocation.

If you ask me which of the three systems is best, I will answer that there are *two points* from which the question must be studied. The one is, what form of church government does the Bible prescribe? The other is, what form best secures obedience to Christ's commandments? The two questions may seem identical, but are very dif-

K

ferent. If the Bible unequivocally pronounced one of the three systems to be the one Christ intended his people to adopt, then there could be no dispute about what all Christians should be. If, however, the Bible has left the question in obscurity, then we must be guided by considerations of propriety and expediency. In reality, no one declares that he can find in the Bible Presbyterianism, Congregationalism, or Episcopalianism, *as they are at the present day.* The practices of the early churches are looked upon as showing what the apostles sanctioned and what we should adopt, and tradition is largely appealed to by the English Church, and by the Roman Catholic Church, as sanctioning their procedure. In truth, however, the most pious, modest, and learned of men are enormously at variance as to what the practices of the ancient church were. About the doings of the churches founded by the Apostles we really know almost nothing. And to affirm, as many do, that at all events we should copy the earliest churches we can get account of, is really to beg the whole question in dispute, for they were not alike in practice, and corruptions and heresies early appeared. It is in truth as difficult to decide which of the ancient churches was the most apostolic, as it is to settle among the modern ones in their great sections. What then is to be done? This, I think. The New Testament has, I believe for the wisest of reasons, avoided giving us a precise and full detail of church organization. It has indicated the great principles on which it should proceed, and left the minor points to be regulated by the varying circumstances of mankind in different countries, under different political constitutions, in different states of intellectual progress, and in different epochs of the world's history. A system *exactly* suited to the Jews of Palestine, would not have accommodated itself to the habits of Englishmen at the present day, neither are any of their systems, utterly unaltered, certainly the best for the primitive inhabitants of a South Sea island. My study of the Bible has led me to be a Congregationalist; it has led others to be Presbyterians and Episcopalians. I have ceased to wonder at this, for only the germ of a church system is to be found there, and I can worship along with either Presbyterians or Episcopalians, whom I believe to be Christians, heartily and delightedly; and there are many among them at at whose feet I could sit as a humble disciple.

You will perhaps say to me here, Surely, a solitary lady like myself is not called upon to decide upon these vexed points? You may well say this, and all the more that you have no voice in governing the church, either as Episcopalian or Presbyterian, for in the Established churches women are powerless. This is true : yet you will see that the activity and prosperity of a religious body may, nay, must, be prodigiously affected by the mode of government. Look, for example, at the power which a single bishop has in England to compel a particular doctrine to be taught to all the thousands in his diocese. Look also at a case like ——'s. His presbytery may stop his preaching, if his opinions do not accord with theirs. The form of church government, therefore, is a very serious matter, and the question which is the best form, deeply concerns all Christians.

I do not think, however, it is the matter which most concerns you at present. God may be worshipped acceptably among all the three bodies referred to. I do not think any one will equally like each, and every Christian should, sooner or later, unite himself with some congregation, Episcopalian, Presbyterian, or Congregational, although he need not narrow himself to constant attendance on one body. There is a question before this, my dear friend. What is the purpose of joining any church? What is implied in joining it? The answers to these questions are to be found in the Bible, and there only. I know you will not take offence at what I write, or mistake my motive; and I would, therefore, suggest earnestly that, before one tries to answer the question, Should I be a Presbyterian? one should ask, Am I a Christian? A form of church government in itself is little, indeed is nothing, without a living faith in Christ. If that has been reached, the rest is easily decided.

So long a time has elapsed since I wrote to you before, and we had so short a conversation, that I know not at what point your religious belief now rests; and I feel unable to give counsel in my ignorance. Perhaps you will kindly tell me whether you now find any of the doctrines of the Church of England unacceptable, or incredible, or doubtful? I shall reply when I receive your answer. Meanwhile, I would advise you to visit both the Established and Episcopalian churches, and judge of the clergymen. Personal edification is a matter of immensely more importance than church forms. . . . . May our blessed Saviour guide us all, and show us his love! I pray for God's blessing on this correspondence, and that his Spirit may teach us his truth.

Yours very truly.

October 20*th,* 1850.

DEAR MRS. Y.,—I write a line of apology and excuse for not sending you a parcel of books. . . . I will delay, however, no longer, but forward with this, two books not referring largely to church systems, but rather to personal religion. They

are both by men of great talent, the teachers
and practisers of a manly piety, such as you, I
think, must desire to see in others, and practise
yourself. Mr. Maurice is an excellent and most
pious person, very free from anything like cant or
fanaticism. He was in early life a Unitarian, and
has reached his present convictions through a
long and resolute struggle, which may make his
conclusions the more interesting to you, as able
to sympathize with such an inward and pro-
tracted striving after truth. He is a very learned
and accomplished scholar, metaphysician, and theo-
logian.

Saturday Evening has always been a very great
favourite with me, as it has also been with all
my intellectual friends. It is the production of
Isaac Taylor, a layman, whose name is less
known than his works, which are famous, such
as the *Natural History of Enthusiasm and
of Fanaticism, The Physical Theory of Another
Life, Ancient Christianity, The Life of Ignatius
Loyola*, etc. He is a large-hearted, liberal,
eloquent man, whose writings have profited and

delighted myself. Tastes, however, differ much : neither of the books I send may be acceptable to yours. I rely, however, upon your frankness in making this known to me, and, sooner or later, I shall hope to hit your liking. The work on Presbyterianism I shall forward as soon as I receive it.

I do not know whether you care for biography. If you do, I should recommend strongly the life of Dr. Arnold, of Rugby. He was a professor at Oxford, a clergyman of the Church of England, and the Head-Teacher of the large public school at Rugby. He was loved and honoured by men of all parties. His life is interesting as that of an eminently able and intellectual man ; but it is further remarkable as the history of one of the most successful and consistent attempts to do that very difficult thing, carry religion into daily life, and make it pervade our secular callings. Most persons, even the most truly religious, find this a difficult thing. They rise from their knees, put away their Bibles or Prayer-books, and begin some worldly duty which quite engrosses them till the hour of religious service comes round again. Which of us will not confess to this, and who will not regret it? This was not the pattern Christ left us, or the apostles imitated from him. There is plainly a way in which a man may be most zealous in his professional or other purely secular dealings, and yet keep a prayerful, worshipful spirit. Now, Arnold succeeded in realizing this more than most men. He was a manly, honest, courageous, generous, and highly-gifted man, whom all partaking of these qualities, or honouring them, must admire. I think you would find his life interesting and profitable. . . . .

I cannot close these hasty lines without feeling the deep responsibility of my task in writing to you on the solemn things which alone occupy this (Sunday) correspondence. You must forgive me if I *seem* to take up the position of teacher, and to pronounce dictatorially on difficult matters. I am so deeply, mournfully conscious of my imperfect resemblance to our blessed Lord and Master, that I count myself but a learner, a very humble disciple and servant of his. If, therefore,

I seem to write as one having authority, set it down only to the necessity for brevity which makes courteous circumlocution inadmissible. And further, if any break occur in my correspondence, be sure it arises from occupation or illness. This is the most anxious season of the year to me, and I may not always be able to write to you when I desire to do it. . . . .

And in all this recommending of books, we must not, my dear friend, forget that the Bible, read alone, with the aid of the parallel passages printed with it, is worth all the commentaries on it. It will interpret itself to all who ask for God's Holy Spirit to guide them into its meaning. . . .

Monday Morning.

I open my letter to acknowledge yours of Saturday, received this morning, as I would not willingly leave it unanswered a day. I did not exactly intend to ask you the question you have answered, but I rejoice that you have sent me so delightful a reply. My purpose was to inquire whether there was any part of the *doctrine* of

Christianity at which you stumbled, not at all to assume the office of confessor, and ask if you were a Christian. But your reply answers the real and supposed question. I gather now that you are not arrested by speculative difficulties in the Christian creed, but by that sense of imperfect imitation of Christ's example which we must all deplore.

I am sure of this, that if we can but utter the publican's prayer, 'God be merciful to me a sinner,' we shall be heard. If we can but say, 'Lord, I believe, help my unbelief,' our faith will be counted to us for righteousness, and will be strengthened and increased. To have got this length is to have got a prodigious length. It is not the worst sign of our being true Christians that we tremble, and yet long to call ourselves such. Only the Holy Spirit can teach us his will, or put it into our hearts to pray to God, or endeavour to do his will. I, my dear friend, will call you Christian, whoever does, and rejoice that we have 'one faith, one Lord, one baptism.'

We must not, however, forget that Christianity

is not a state into which we pass *at once*, and, being once in which, we are at liberty to stand still. Christianity is 'a life,' which is constantly progressive. We are never, as St. Paul tells us, to think that 'we have attained, or are already perfect.' We are to 'forget the things that are behind, and to press on to those that are before.' We are also 'to work out our salvation with fear and trembling,' and to 'make our calling and election sure.' When we find so holy a man and so eminent a Christian as Paul ever striving to realize Christianity better and better, constantly finding that, as he advanced in knowledge of Christ, it was possible and desirable to know his Saviour better, what ought such weak disciples as we to think of the necessity laid upon us to go on,—on,—on? If Christ indeed be God, *infinite* in all his attributes, not even eternity, still less time, will suffice to exhaust his excellencies, so that we shall have to say we have learned all. We are at best babes in Christ, and have to grow up to the full stature of manhood in him. It will take our earthly lives to do this, and will delightfully employ all eternity.

On this and such subjects I write with far more delight than on questions of church government, which have but a secondary interest for me. I must, however, reluctantly conclude, as I have a large packet of letters to answer.

October 27th, 1850.

WITH regard to the sad presentiment which you tell me fills your mind as to what you will die of, we must be content to leave in God's hand our mortal disease, and the details of our death-bed. I may well dread consumption, for my twin-brother and two cousins, my dearest friends, died of it; but I feel that, if I were allowed to choose my way of death, I should not (having regard to the moral and spiritual aspects of death) know what mode of dying to fix upon, and I rejoice to leave it to Him, who sent me into the world, to call me from it in his own time and way. My dear friend, we are bad judges of what is best for us, and often dread what is furthest from us. The great matter is to realize the spirit of the beautiful Evening Hymn of the English Church, and to live so that health or disease shall equally find us resigned to God's will. His command is very plain, that 'whatever our hand findeth to do, we are to do it with all our might,' and we are to be 'diligent in business,' asking his blessing on our work. We may fill our hearts with apprehensions which will not be realized, and be tried with afflictions we never anticipated. There is no rest or comfort to be got out of our own imaginings, whether they take a sombre or a vivid colouring. I say this, deeply sympathizing with the tendency to anticipate evil, which is en-grained in my nature. It should be disowned, however: we must fight against it. The cure is to be found in our Saviour's command, 'Take no thought for the morrow;' in the assurance of St. Paul, that nothing can separate us from 'the love of God in Christ Jesus our Lord;' and in St. John's declaration, that 'perfect love casteth out fear.' The New Testament is full of such passages to overflowing. We are assured that all things work together for good to those who love God; we are told also that Christ's grace (*i.e.*, his benignant favour) 'is sufficient for us,' or will serve for all our trials; and that 'his strength will be made perfect in our weakness.' We should, therefore, pray for strength, for help, for faith, and most when dark apprehensions crowd upon us; for this world and the whole universe are God's, and Christ's, and by no possibility can anything occur without his knowledge and permission; nor can disease, or sorrow, or other trial of any kind, transfer us into a region where God's control ceases, or make us acquainted with agonies with which our Saviour cannot sympathize. The last two verses of the eighth chapter of the Epistle to the Romans assure us of this in the fullest and most cheering terms.

From this the transition is direct to another matter to which I would specially refer. You feel that God is just as well as merciful, and that you may forfeit his mercy if you offend his justice. I think you may rejoice that you have a heart made

sensitive to the demands of God's justice. Only
the Holy Spirit can give us this grace, and, seeing that hundreds around us die without any sense
of the just demands upon them, of Him before
whom they must appear to answer for the deeds
done in the body, we may feel thankful that we
are clear at least of this sin, and have some recognition, however inadequate, of the truth, that
the Judge of all the earth must and will do right.
Here, however, we must not stop. Most truly
have you settled that the wilful breaking of God's
laws is incompatible with his requirements from
his creatures. St. Paul warns us that we must
not sin that grace may abound. In other words,
we are not to think that the long-suffering of God,
and his compassion for sinners, and his willingness to forgive all penitents their sins, entitle us
to transgress *deliberately*, counting upon his forgiveness.

On the other hand, however, we must for ever
forswear all attempt to make out a righteousness
for ourselves. Assuredly we are in the wrong if
we practise any known sin. This is to build up

our faith with one hand, and knock it down with the other. Deliberately and continuously to break what we believe to be a positive command of our Saviour's, who has required us to show our love to him 'by keeping his commandments,' is to mock him, and make hypocrites of ourselves. But we are never to doubt our Lord and Master's willingness, readiness, and sufficiency to forgive us, however often and deeply we have sinned. This is *the great truth* of the Bible, the mighty central fact which makes it a message of mercy to men; and I would urge this characteristic of God's revelation upon you. St. Paul reproaches the Galatians : 'Are ye so foolish? having *begun* in the Spirit, are ye now *made perfect* in the flesh?' In another place, Christ is referred to as the 'Author and Finisher of our faith.' In Revelation he is called 'the Alpha and Omega, the Beginning and the Ending.' 'He *ever* liveth to make intercession for us.' 'If any man sin,' says St. John in his First Epistle, 'we have an Advocate with the Father, Jesus Christ the Righteous.' The parable of the unjust judge is to teach us that we

L

are to 'pray without ceasing,' and that God will never close his ears to our prayers. Another parable was spoken to remind us 'that we are to pray, and not to faint,' *i.e.*, not to lose heart and stop praying. The disciple who asked our Saviour how often he should. forgive his erring brother, was told not to be content with forgiving him seven times, but to do it 'seventy times seven,' to show how 'plenteous in mercy' the Saviour himself was.

From these passages, and many others, we are assuredly entitled and intended to learn that we may always acceptably pray to God, and that the blessed announcement, 'If we confess our sins, he is faithful and just to forgive us our sins, and to cleanse us from all unrighteousness,' is an assurance that we shall never be refused a hearing by our God and Father in Christ Jesus.

I would say, therefore, to you as I say to myself, the more you feel the inability to keep God's law, pray the more that you may have an interest in the death of Christ, have his righteousness imputed to you, and be filled with his Spirit.

No son or daughter of Adam has entered heaven with a holiness of his or her own. We should *despise* God's law, if it were such a commandment as we could keep. The greatest virtue of the most saintly mortal must fall immeasurably short of the requirements of a law which has no degrees, but demands of all who profess to obey it absolutely perfect obedience. It is Christ who must obey it for us. We cannot obey it for ourselves. He can, and if we have faith in him, it will be imputed to us for righteousness, and, 'as he became sin for us who knew no sin, we shall be counted the righteousness of God in him.' Therefore, my dear friend, let us ever pray. Whether ill or well, desponding or rejoicing, prosperous or in adversity, we always need to pray, we shall always profit by prayer. And inasmuch as it was not the righteous, but sinners that Christ came to die for, and to call to repentance, we may rest assured that, however sinful, we are free to address our petitions to God, and that our blessed Redeemer, who knows our frailties, will compassionate us, and intercede for even 'the chief of sinners' who implores his aid. Do not, therefore, let a sense of God's justice interrupt your prayers. He has permitted, invited, nay, commanded '*all* men to pray;' he has promised his Holy Spirit to teach us how to pray ; he has assured us that he is 'ever well pleased' with the mighty Intercessor in whose name we pray. Therefore, my dear friend, pray, and, earnestly striving to walk in the ways of the Lord, leave all to him. He always answers prayer; not, perhaps, in the way we expect or wish, but he is a prayer-hearing, prayer-answering God, who never slumbers nor sleeps, who is always ready to be petitioned, and, even before our requests are offered, is ready with an answer to them.

In my own humble prayers, I will not forget you ; neither, I know, will Mrs. ——. I shall pray for you, and G., and all your young family. It is a blessed thing to be prayed for. Forget me not in your prayers.

Your sincere friend.

November 17*th*, 1850.

DEAR Mrs. Y.—H.'s book has arrived quite safely, and both your letters ; and I will refer at once to the point with which they are mainly occupied. You referred to it in a former letter, and I neglected to take notice of it. This was not from any reluctance to tell you my mind freely on the matter, but only from haste and inadvertence.

I can heartily assure you that I entirely sympathize with your reluctance to talk about the state of your soul with Mrs. ——, or Miss ——. I know the style of conversation you refer to, and I do not like it, nor do I think it likely to be profitable in *many* cases. The former lady I know very slightly, the latter not at all. I can well believe that both are—as I know the first is—true and earnest Christians, and I do not doubt that some persons find it conducive to spiritual progress to make their own experiences the subject of constant conversation. I would not, therefore, condemn the practice as necessarily injurious and unwise, but assuredly it is not a Christian duty, and to many minds—to none more than my own—it would be utterly destructive of that solemn reverential fear of God which is the beginning of wisdom, and that adoring love of Christ our Saviour, which fills the heart to the casting out of all unworthy fear, but which is not to be uttered. You will understand, then, that there is not a point on which we can be more at one than this; but I will say more. I should be very sorry to make my personal tastes as to religious studies or duties a standard for you or any other person. I can assure you, however, that in your reluctance to make every acquaintance a father or mother confessor, all I most esteem as devout Christians would participate. My mother and sisters, who, I truly believe, are behind few in earnest, intelligent faith in Christ, would shrink in horror from such conversations as you report. My eldest sister, who was remarkable for her sagacity, prudence, intellectual accomplishments, moral courage, and, withal, meekness and patience, would, I believe, have almost gone the length of reproving any one who, on short acquaintance, touched on personal religious experience.

I have not, for my own part, more than some three friends with whom I converse on such matters. Two of them I knew for years before we exchanged confidences, and the third is a clergyman, to whom, more than to any living person, I am indebted for help in religious things. I count it a great privilege to have such friends ; it is impossible I should have many, and only at intervals do I converse with them on religion, and rarely in the way of curious inquisition into our respective experiences. I think most of my religious friends have a reluctance, similar to my own, to talk of the kind you refer to. In truth, I am afraid I am so much at one with you that I feel the risk of pressing the point too far. . . .

Monday Evening.

This length I had got last night when the very evil which is the subject of remark befel me. I discourage Sunday visits, feeling that a seventh part of my time is not too much to devote to the worship of God. A cold, however, kept me from church, and a friend, who missed me from my

pew, called to ask for me, nor could I with any
sort of grace get rid of him, though much per-
plexed about his visit. He remained to supper,
disputing with me concerning this Bull of the
Pope's, and deprived you of this letter. This has
occasioned me vexation, for I knew that I should
be occupied to-day till dinner-time, without an interval to address you. What I was about to refer
to, when interrupted, was the advantage which
there is in having religious friends of one's own
sex, as well as of the other, and that you would
find thoughtful, intelligent, devout women, able to
assist and instruct you in religious matters where
men could not help. I have known women of
various ages and degrees of culture, and unlike in
amount of refinement, who were to myself teachers
in spiritual things. To my eldest sister, I was
deeply indebted for furthering in the Christian life,
and that long after I came to man's estate. Most
of the Christian ladies I knew, including her, are
deceased, and I feel it a great loss to miss their
assistance, encouragement, and monition in religious studies and works. It may be that in ——

you may find such; perhaps even the parties you refer to, may prove on a longer acquaintance, *in spite of* their style of conversation, serviceable. If not, in due time I will hope and pray that you may meet some Christian lady, as earnest and intelligent and devout as she is reserved and cautious in ordinary intercourse in her references to religion, and till you do, I see nothing else for it but courteously to discourage mere everyday talk about personal experiences, and to turn the conversation, if it cannot be suppressed, into some wholesome channel, such as the lives of great and good men, the best systems of Sabbath-school teaching, the most efficient means of serving the poor, etc. Some allowance must be made for —— . . . . . mixing chiefly with a certain class of religious people. She has, if I mistake not, been brought up in a circle considerably unlike yours, and probably misunderstands you, as it may be, to some extent, you misunderstand her. Time may bring about a perception of mutual objects of interest; and common sympathies, and a better acquaintance with each other, may enable both of you to avoid subjects which are on either side distasteful. This, however, must plainly be a work of time; and for the present, I say, as I did at the commencement of this letter, you are justified in disrelishing the style of conversation you refer to, and are disobeying no religious or moral law in avoiding it.

I am glad you like Arnold. He was too zealous a worker to be a great writer. It would scarcely be fair to compare him with Southey, so far as style is concerned. The latter had a rare command over language, such as not one man in a thousand attains. His profession was to write, and he trained himself to this and *to nothing else*, and constantly practised it. I suppose he had written some hundred times more prose than Arnold ever did, besides all his poetry. Southey is one of my great favourites. I have read him with delight ever since I was a boy, and only finished his correspondence on Friday. There is nothing you can say in praise of his style which I will not re-echo; but he is a rare writer, and we cannot expect to meet many who have a style to match his. Arnold had all the toils of a schoolmaster to occupy and distract him. His heart was set on certain high moral achievements, and the realization of certain great truths, for which he struggled. Even if he had had the natural gifts of Southey, he never had his training or practice in writing; and, moreover, like all practical men, he was more bent on doing a thing than solicitous how it should be done. Many of his sermons were finished just as the bell tolled for church, and he had no leisure to think of the most graceful words in which an earnest thought should be spoken. A similar remark applies to his *History of Rome*, where its substance is admirable, but its clothing, though excellent, not so beautiful as it would have been in a poet's hands.

The lesson of his life was the success with which he made religion sanctify everything, and did all 'to the glory of God.' Is it not cheering also to know that such a man was of like passions and infirmities with ourselves; and hoped, and feared, and trembled as we do? We must not hope to escape this. It is our appointed element. 'Work out your salvation,' says the apostle, 'with fear

and trembling ;' and again, 'ye have need of patience.' The Saviour would not pray that his
disciples might be taken out of the world, but only
that they 'might be kept from the evil' in it. The
glorified spirits whom John saw in vision, clothed
in white, and with palms in their hands, had come
through 'great tribulation.' When we think of the
trials which He underwent who was 'a man of sorrows and acquainted with grief,' and call to remembrance that solemn, nay awful, unspeakably awful
scene in the garden of Gethsemane, shall we wonder if we suffer, or that our hearts are often ex-
ceedingly sorrowful, and our spirits utterly dis-
composed? It would be an ill omen for us if
unbroken peace reigned in our souls; if whilst all
the saints of old, and all the holy men of all
Christian countries, have been found the prey of
an internal conflict, that solemnized their spirits in
their lightest moods, we were free from fears. Nor
is this condition incompatible with the promise
which the Bible makes that we shall have 'rest
in Christ,' enjoy 'a peace that passeth all understanding,' and have 'joy and peace in believing.'

These *are* granted in measure sufficient to even the least of all saints; but only in proportion to the intensity of our faith in Christ, and the earnest reality of our belief in him, can be our share of peace and rest and joy. And only consider what our aim is, even to be perfectly holy, to know Christ, to be filled with the fulness of God, to have our whole natures transformed, so that we may become sinless creatures, the true image of our Creator. Striving to attain this, must we not feel at each forward step, how vast the territory yet before us is, and how much quicker we might traverse it? All eternity will not exhaust the knowledge of Him who is infinite, so that we shall say, 'There is nothing more to be learned of God; we have become all-knowing and all-holy as he is;' how much less can the worship of God for a few years on this earth beget in our minds the assurance that we may seek repose! We may yet faint or fail, lose patience, yield to temptation, be overcome of evil, and become great transgressors. To 'watch and pray' must to the last be our motto.

Religious people are often accused of hypocrisy
or fanaticism, because, in private letters or diaries,
they are found mourning over the commission of
what we call some *venial* sin.   Yet in this accusation they are often greatly wronged.   The more
sensitive we become to the justice of God's demands upon us, and the more alive we are to
the spotlessness of his holiness, the more sensitive
must we grow to our own sinfulness ; and the holier
we become, the lower estimate we shall form of our
own holiness.   If that great saint, the apostle John,
declared that ' if we say we have no sin, we deceive
ourselves, and the truth is not in us,' must not all,
the saintliest and the vilest, think with shame and
grief of sin, as hateful to God, and dishonour-
ing to themselves ?   An irreligious person will probably think a hasty word, an equivocating reply,
a neglect of duty of a small kind, and the like, matters to be dismissed as quickly as possible from his
thoughts.   But to a Christian, remembering the
command, ' Be ye holy, as I am holy,' can the
slightest transgression be other than a cause of
sorrow and humiliation ?

We cannot therefore but expect the lives of good men, like Arnold, to abound in such passages as you refer to ; and whilst immense allowance must be made for differences in men's temperaments, which lead some to gloom and others to gaiety, I feel certain that no true follower of the Lord Jesus Christ will be found who is not the subject of many alternations of joy and sorrow, and daily has occasion to mingle self-reproaches with rejoicings.

I will not write more at present. I have been too prolix on this point. The life of Christ in the Gospels is the biography of biographies. It is the corrective to set against men's lives. He left us in *all* things 'an example, that we should follow his steps;' and only through much struggle against sloth and pride and folly, and all other forms of evil, can we, sustained by him, trace his footprints, and tread in them. We shall die sinners as we have lived sinners, struggling to the last, saved by him who, as he is the Author, is also the Finisher of our faith, who has assured us that he will never leave us nor forsake us, and that he will be with his people 'always, even to the end.' . . . .

December 22d, 1850.

MY DEAR MRS. Y.,—I cannot allow another week
to pass away without writing to you a few lines.
This is a season when all British people exchange
kind greetings, and especially kind ones should pass
between Christians. You will find Christmas a very
different matter in Scotland from what it is in England.   We suffered so much as a people from the
Romish Church in older days, and from Charles
II., who persecuted in the name of the Church of
England, that at the Reformation and at the Re-
volution, we went to the opposite extreme, and
denuded our church-services of those festivals which
the other churches of Europe have retained. Christmas, accordingly, is in Scotland entirely divested
of a religious character, except among the Roman
Catholics and Episcopalians.   I will not ask
whether this is well or ill. What I wish most to
say is, that I rejoice to find that that very interesting Christmas device ' *die Tannenbaum,*' which our
good German friends have taught us to admire, is
to delight Georgy's eyes. Whatever may be thought
of the religious services of Christmas, there are few

of us who will find fault with a holiday. And yet, do you know, there is something mournful in recurring festivals which, year by year, render more manifest the sorrows which have been felt since they were last celebrated. I have long ceased to think of them otherwise than with a certain dread, arising from the many sad events which have characterized our family history. There were once eleven of us; there are now only four, and I remember the deaths of five, besides that of my father, and of two cousins who were brought up with us, and died in our presence. My birthday is never mentioned in our circles, for it only brings back to my mother the memory of my twin-brother, who was still more delicate than I am, and very dearly loved by her; and there are many other black days which will come back draped in mourning; and the longer one lives, they gather the more abundantly behind, so that we keep no saints' days or family festivals of any kind. This, however, is not well. We know it to be best for *us*, and our sorrows are sanctified by many blessed hopes and remembrances. Had we children among us, I should think our gravity (for we are not gloomy) improper and unfair towards them; and I wish to give you a practical proof of this by contributing to adorn your Christmas tree, if a few twigs can be spared us. . . . Children should be made as happy as possible. A sorrowful childhood darkens the whole later life, and stamps a peculiarity on the whole character. Poor Georgy will have enough of this without its being otherwise wrought into him; but the sorrows God sends, he blesses 'and changes into joys for those who acknowledge him. . . . To Georgy I always come back with peculiar sympathy; and I have added, for his special delectation, a book on Natural History, which will continue to interest him after the Tree is forgotten. Much of my delight as a child arose out of natural history. It gives food to the imagination, and tempers the fairy books, of which too many cannot be given to children.

I am glad you liked the *Address.*[1]   I hope

[1] *On the Sacredness of Medicine as a Profession:* An Address to Medical Students.

in the *Life of John Reid*[1] to speak more earnestly
to students of medicine than I have ever yet been
able to do.. Let me say, however, that I was
grieved you had found anything to excite a painful feeling in the *Address.* I would say thus
much on the matter : I know well, profoundly
well, what it is to yearn after sympathy and long
for regard. So strong is the feeling in me, that
I do not know what I would not give to be the
friend of some living men, provided circumstances
sanctioned intercourse between us. And as for
the dead, the great dead, I claim friendship with
them all, and read every biography of a notice-
able man I can find, and write biographies with
my heart in the work.

Nevertheless, long ago, I have realized that on
this earth ' time and chance '—as King Solomon
says—' happen to all men.' It is but a small
number we can see of those we might long to see
and know ; and of those we do see, many are
offended at our manner, and we at theirs. For I

---

[1] *Life of Dr. John Reid*, Professor of Anatomy at St.
Andrews.

have observed that we hate many worthy people, because their ways are unlike our ways, although we respect them, and, could we get beyond their manners, would even love them. And I know people who keep clear of me, yet respect me more than others who are very kind. It must be so in this ill-assorted world. And we ought not to stake our happiness on winning the friendship of any one. Sir Walter Scott, who knew human nature well, held that there was no man from whom something might not be learned; and we often feel that we should, and that we might, love all men ; and then again the blackness and the darkness, the meanness and unworthiness, of our own hearts, and their lurid reflections from the souls of others, make us despise ourselves, and still more the ignoble around us.

I think the wisest thing is to try to love those about us, and so to commend ourselves to their loves. God has apportioned to each of us a circle of relationships. We may think we could have chalked out a better for ourselves; but we cannot escape from the one he_ has placed us within, and there we should practise the blessed precept, that it is better and more blessed to give than to receive. We should bestow our affection on all it will benefit, and be as unexacting as we can in return. And, above all, my dear friend, we should look to this, that we give Christ the first place in our affections. We are self-condemned if we read other men's lives, and do not read his; if we honour his imperfect resemblances and poor copies, and do not honour him; if we delight in what a Shakspere, a Bacon, or a Southey wrote, and do not find pleasure in his Divine words. If we love him, he will love us, and our love is the evidence that he has first loved us. 'To make idols, and to find them clay,' is, according to Mrs. Hemans, the lot of woman; she might have added, of man also.

For the reverse of this I strive. I have seen all my idols overturned, and long now only to enshrine my Saviour in my heart, assured that all unlawful affections will be banished from his presence, and that all lawful ones will be exalted and intensified by it. I know no remedy but this; I would recommend it to you. He that sticketh closer than a brother, that is with us to the end, that is where two or three are gathered together in his name, can fill our hearts, though no one else fill them; can invest our earthly affections and human sympathies with deeper, more solemn, and more sanctified regards. If the head of the republic of Science, Letters, and Arts should be the greatest Professor of these, who shall be the Head of the sympathies, the affections, and the deep-seated yearnings of the heart, but the one only sinless perfect Man, the sympathizing High Priest, the mighty Intercessor, and the all-prevailing Redeemer? Without him all earthly love is precarious and transitory; with him the dreariest heart knows a peaceful sunshine.

I will not say more. Three times have I been interrupted, and I have had to scrawl the close of this. The sum of it all is, that if Christ be the centre of our affections, other objects of regard will naturally group themselves at their due distances round him.

Yours very truly.

P.S.—Give G. all kindly, friendly, hearty Christmas wishes. In another letter, I'll tell you about my poetical projects.

To GEORGY Y.[1]

MY DEAR GEORGY,—I have learned with very great regret and sorrow, that you are again suffering severely. Long before I saw you, I had an interest in you for the sake of my dear friends, your mamma and papa ; and when I saw you in —— I took an interest in you for your own sake, and liked you all the better that you bore the same Christian name as papa and myself. It was a bond of connexion between us three. I did not then think I should soon have to feel sympathy for you as about to be a great sufferer. It has pleased God, however, no doubt for wise purposes, to send you sore affliction, and to try your courage and patience by much pain. I know from personal experience, how difficult a thing it

---

[1] An invalid boy, son of the lady to whom the preceding letters are addressed.

is to endure long-protracted agony, and I never
think of you without earnestly wishing that I knew
some wonderful medicine which would make you
altogether well again.   Alas ! neither papa, nor
Mr. ——, nor I, wise as we think ourselves, can
devise such a remedy, and we must all look on
at your suffering, and mourn that we can do so
little to relieve you.   But what none of us can do,
God can do.   The blessed Saviour came to this
world, and lived a life of poverty, reproach, and
humiliation ; submitted to be mocked and dishonoured, cruelly tortured and put to death on the
cross, that he might put away sin (which is the
cause of suffering being in this earth at all), by
the sacrifice of himself.   He atoned to God for
the despising and transgressing of his laws, the indifference to his will, and the forgetfulness of his
kindness towards them, of which all men are guilty.
For God is our Father in heaven, and we should
love and honour and obey him as children, whereas we have hated and dishonoured and disobeyed
him ; and had not Christ atoned to our heavenly
Father for our crimes, we must have endured, each

one of us, the awful wrath of our offended God. Christ, however, has suffered in our room, the just for the unjust; he has endured the wrath of God for us; and if we will only repent of our sins, and confess them before God, and beseech him for the sake of what our Saviour has suffered, to forgive us, to be reconciled to us, to love us as children, and put in our hearts his Holy Spirit, so that we may become haters of sin, and lovers of holiness, he will grant our prayer, and make all things work together for our good. But when we say good, we must not decide in our hearts what is best for us. Invalids, like you and me, are apt to think that nothing could be so good for us as to be strong and stout and cheerful, and to ask God only for health and worldly comfort. Yet our Father in heaven may see that if he gave us health and wealth and ease, we should only be tempted to forget him, and involve ourselves in great transgression and suffering. And so he may prefer to send us sickness and pain, and confine us to our chambers, where we shall be free from temptation, and be able to think in quietness of our own sins, and of God's justice and holiness. If you ask mamma, she will read to you the first eleven verses of the 12th chapter of the Hebrews. You will see from them how mistaken we may be in thinking that God does not love us, because he sends us suffering : 'Whom the Lord loveth he chasteneth, and scourgeth every son whom he receiveth.'

And we must not forget, my dear Georgy, what when young often escapes our remembrance, that it may not be God's purpose to grant us length of days. Those, indeed, who, like you and me, have been long and often ill, should lay to account that the probability is the other way. It may please God to restore you to health, and give you many years to enjoy it upon this earth ; but it may be his intention to summon you to himself, and none of us know how soon the call may come to any among us ; only to invalids like us the warning to 'prepare to meet our God' is addressed with a loudness and a distinctness which it is not to others. Perhaps when we are hoping most to be better, and thinking what we

shall do when we are well, God, out of his very
love to us, is about, for ever, to put an end to our
sufferings, and take us to himself. And if, my
dear Georgy, he were to send one of his angels to
whisper in your ear that he would very soon send
for you, how would you receive the news? It is a
mournful thing to leave parents, and sisters, and
brother, and kind friends, but 'to be with Christ
is far better.' This world at best is a sorrowful
world. Its highest joys are unabiding and un-
satisfying; its cares are many. It is full of wrong
and abounding in temptations. In heaven there
is no sin, no wrong, no pain, no fear, no sorrow,
no crying; all tears are wiped away from the eyes
of its blessed inhabitants. Often do I long to be
there, beside my dear brothers and sisters, away
from this weary sinful world. Fervently do I pray
that in his own good time and way, when he sees
it to be best, God will take you to that happy
place.

But if we are to reach heaven we must be holy.
God will make no unrepentant sinner happy. He
offers all men forgiveness for Christ's sake; but if

they will not accept this, if they despise his mercy, if they offend his Holy Spirit, and prefer their own ways to obedience to his supreme and righteous will, he will send them from his presence into everlasting woe.   Blessed be his name, that need be the fate of none of us.   'Come unto me,' we read, '*all* ye that labour and are heavy laden, and I will give you rest.'   'Ask, and it shall be given you ; seek, and ye shall find; knock, and it shall be opened unto you.'   'If any man lack wisdom, let him ask of God, that giveth to all liberally, and upbraideth not ; and it *shall* be given him.'

Pray then, my dear Georgy, to God.   A long and formal prayer is not necessary.   An earnest request, uttered reverently, will reach his ear, and be answered as certainly as the lengthened elaborate prayer of a whole congregation.   Ask him for Christ's sake to forgive and bless you, to give you his Spirit, and make you a child of his; and whilst you pray for- relief from pain and sickness, and weakness and weariness, pray not less earnestly for patience and submission, and that you may be able to submit to his will towards you.

Above all, ask to be made like unto Christ, for he only of all men was perfect. He never sinned nor offended God ; he yielded to him an entire and joyful obedience ; he delighted to do his will, and he has 'left us an example that we should follow his steps.' And further, this only sinless, holy man, was on this earth a far greater sufferer than any of his sinful, unholy brethren. God laid upon him 'the iniquity of us all.' He was 'a man of sorrows, and acquainted with grief.' All sufferers can look to him as one who knew, by personal experience, what pain, and misery, and agony are. ' He was in *all* points tempted (that is, tried or exercised) like as we are,' so that we may be certain he can enter into our feelings, and sympathize with us. This, however, would be but a small matter if he could not help us. He is in heaven, invisible to us, and we are apt to think that the sympathy of our friends about us is worth a great deal more than that of an unseen, far-off friend. But this great Saviour thought it not robbery to be equal with God. He was himself the Son of God, the 'only begotten of the Father.' In a wonderful and mysterious way he united in himself what no other being has ever done, all the qualities of a perfect man and all the attributes of God. He could never have atoned for our sins had he been *only* man, for a mere man could not do more, even if innocent like Adam before he fell, than justify himself to God. But Christ was able, because he was divine, to suffer for the whole world, and make a propitiation for its sins. We can thus trust in him as one 'mighty to save,' who can help us with all the power of God, and who is superior to all human beings, to all angels, and to all devils, and can assist us against every temptation, and defend us from every assailant. Therefore it was, dear Georgy, that I contrasted our inability to help you with that of God; for Christ is God; and if you hearken to the second chapter of the Hebrews, and the last four verses of the fourth, you will see how able and how willing our glorified Saviour is to succour us. He is now exalted at the right hand of God, a Prince and Saviour, a Great High Priest, who has offered up a mighty sacrifice, but one who can, in all his exaltation, be 'touched with the feeling of our infirmities,' and 'who ever liveth to make intercession for us.' Trust in him. On earth he said, 'Suffer little children to come unto me, and forbid them not, for of such is the kingdom of heaven.' Pray to him. If he does not heal your malady, he will give you faith in him, patience, peace of mind, and contentment. If he thinks it best for you, he will restore you to health; but he may think it better to take you to himself, and your days in this earth perhaps are numbered. Leave all to him. He, if you trust in him, will 'never leave nor forsake you,' and, whether you live or die, it will be well with you.

Your affectionate friend.

June 8th, 1851.

DEAR MRS. Y.,—I very confidently calculated on being able to write you four weeks ago; but I was disappointed, and felt that I must have forfeited so totally your regard by my apparent negligence and forgetfulness, that I resolved to send no more

apologies, but to wait till I could write. The cause
of my silence was simply that I had undertaken to
conduct a Bible-class in the absence of the teacher.
This has occupied all the leisure of the last four
Sundays, whilst an unusual amount of laboratory
work has swallowed up the week-days. Gladly
do I now fulfil my tardy promise, although I cannot say that I have anything very special to write.
You must consider this rather a re-commence-
ment of correspondence than anything else. I
am in better health than I have been in for a
long time. I cannot say that I am stronger, but
I am more free from pain than for a very long
interval. I am only, however, slowly recovering
from the mental exhaustion of last winter, during which my brain was completely overwrought.
This is the chief reason why I have not written
to you : I was sick of pen and paper. I
am sorry to find that Y. has been poorly latterly.
The summer weather will, I trust, give him a
firmer hold on life and health, and conduce to
his complete recovery, so far at least as freedom
from pain is concerned. If, like me, he goes

halting to his grave, he can join with me in thinking how many great and good men have done so
before us. . . . . And if it rather please God to
take my dear namesake to himself, we shall rejoice in the hope that he will answer our prayers,
and that Georgy will go to be with Christ, 'which is
far better.' I have been much struck recently with
the statement of our Saviour, in reference to the
resurrection of the dead, in the conversation
which he had with the Sadducees, where he says,
'Neither *can* they die any more.' The *can* is so
much more expressive than *will* or *shall* would
have been. Death has become an impossibility
for the resurrected ones. There is something
doubly solemn in the thought. The happy dead
are no longer to 'die daily,' never again to
change their state, to undergo no further mighty
metamorphosis, but only to perfect that exalted,
angel-like nature which is to be the character of
their new bodies. And the unhappy dead! Will
there be a bitterer drop in their cup of woe than
that they cannot die? What longings for anni-
hilation must resound throughout the regions of

N

despair! Eternal dying is to us something inconceivable, and the Bible systematically avoids all *detailed* reference to the unseen world. But, however we understand it, a conscious dying must be an unspeakably awful thing; a continuous, reproducing, unending misery; a dreadful tragedy for ever acting itself, and only ending that it may begin anew.

I do not know whether you have ever witnessed death. Upon the whole, I incline to think that the most painful thing in watching the last moments of a dear friend is not the spectacle of suffering or weakness, but the dread suspense at that interval when consciousness has departed, and yet death has not arrived. The dying seem neither in this world nor in the next. We cannot comfort them; they cannot address us. They are shut off from communication with us, and yet they are not with God. If there be a period when evil spirits tempt God's saints, this, I think, must be preeminently the time. They have entered on the threshold of the world of spirits, and are assaulted at its very entrance. Yet why refer so specially to all this? I have been thinking aloud rather than writing to purpose. Such speculations as those I have referred to, are all forgotten in the remembrance that, at the moment when we can do least for the dying, our Saviour, who has promised to be with his people ' even to the end,' can and does do most for them. He has the keys of death and of the invisible world; he has gone before them, and prepared a place for them, and he will come again and receive them to himself. There is a favourite saying among the Methodists, ' that man's extremity is God's opportunity;' that when we can do least God does most. And after all, this is true of all seasons and conditions of mankind. It is not merely on a death-bed that we owe all to Christ. He is the author or beginner, as well as the finisher or ender, of our faith. We are only safe following in his steps, and we shall find his footprints if we seek for them, all through this world, all through the green pastures by the quiet waters, where the great Shepherd will lead his redeemed and ransomed flock.

' To know Christ, and to be known of him :' if

we could realize in our own experience these words, and feel that such a living bond of trust, and love, and confidence, united us to him, as unites us to an earthly brother whom we greatly honour, and to whom we have been unspeakably indebted, whilst we realize that this friend is God himself, how happy should we be! It will take all eternity to master the full meaning of these words, but we may begin to interpret them here.

June 22*d*, 1851.

. . . I am struck by what you say of your presentiment of death. In itself it is nothing, for I have known it fail signally in many cases. It may be, however, that God has put into your heart a warning that you may make ready, and, though I discourage in myself, and would in others, the habit of watching emotions, which often leads to our transmuting fears into predictions, yet we are all so certainly doomed to die, and every illness is so unquestionably an additional warning that we must soon put off the body, that we can never do amiss in keeping death before us. The poet has said, that 'what we fondly wish, we fain believe,' and it is as true that what we greatly dread we fain believe. Perhaps your presentiment partakes both of hope and fear : wish to be in the unchanging sinless world ; dread of the awful gate through which alone it can be reached, and of the judgment that is to follow death ; mingled with sorrow at the thought that you must part from those you most dearly love on this earth.

Abstaining from all analysis of the exact nature of the anticipation of death at no very distant period which you entertain, we may, at least, most truly accept it as a message from God. It was remarked to me once by my mother, that the valley of the shadow of death, spoken of in the twenty-third Psalm, does not refer, as is generally supposed, *merely* to the closing days of our life, but to our entire mortal existence, and I believe it is the true version. We are born into the valley which, like some long, narrow gorge between two hills, is widest at the entrance, and narrows to the gate which opens into the world of spirits. The only difference between the passage of one as compared with another through that valley, is in regard to the swiftness with which it is traversed. An irresistible all-compelling force is for ever carrying us onwards into the increasing darkness of the narrowing path, and the utter darkness of the terminating door-way.   We need, indeed, no presentiment to assure us that we must soon die ; only, if we are haunted with the conviction that we shall soon depart, we ought to give the more heed to preparation for the great change.   I remember that, before I could find any personal interest in the promises of the Bible, and especially in early life, I used to indulge my fancy in bright visions of the glories of heaven, and there were few parts of the New Testament I read with so much delight as those in the book of Revelation describing the happy land.   But when I came to lie very near the gates of death, I found that the engrossing concern was not what are the glories of heaven, but shall I ever reach it ?   I believe that few Christians with death at hand, think much of the glorious pictures of heaven, which,

when death was far off, occupied their minds; not
that they doubt the truth of these, for if 'eye hath
not seen, nor ear heard, neither have entered into
the heart of man the things which God has prepared for them that love him,' we may be certain
that we cannot over-picture the delights of heaven.
Dying Christians fix their thoughts upon Christ;
and you and I, my dear friend, if we think ourselves warned to die, more than others, will condemn ourselves if we do not make him the more
the object of our thoughts that death occupies
them. It is an awful reality, which will, I am sure,
from the half glimpses I have had of it, exceed all
conceptions of its true nature. Even the holiest
Christians, when *suddenly* summoned to die, have
shrunk with terror from the last enemy, and we
should guard against those poetical pictures of
death as a sleep, which writers of fiction love to
draw. I have myself at an earlier period longed
for death, but now I more frequently lay to heart
our Saviour's prayer for his disciples, which was,
not that his Father should take them out of the
world, but that he should keep them from the evil

that is in it.   This is now my prayer.   Grace to
live from day to day an increasingly Christian life,
without being inordinately anxious about the morrow.   Faith in Christ, as the only and all-sufficient
Saviour for us, and more success in imitating the
example of him who is Lord and Master, are and
must be the great aims of every Christian, and if
reached and realized, will prepare him equally
for death and life.   The development of faith and
hope, the progressive sanctification of our spirits,
and a closer brotherhood to Christ, are to be attained, are indeed only to be attained, by reading
God's Word, and by earnest prayer to him.   The
wondrous things he can and will teach out of his
law, those who fulfil the Saviour's command to
'search the Scriptures,' all who have obeyed it
bear witness to.   The answers he sends to prayer
are not less certain or less precious.   It is never
safe for us to brood too much inwardly, or gaze
into our hearts expecting to find comfort there.
It is always safe, profitable, and pleasant to look
out of ourselves to God, and his provisions for
enabling us to do this are his revealed Word, and

prayer. To commit to memory every day a single verse of a chapter containing a striking truth, is an excellent thing even for the oldest of us grown-up children. When sore sickness or great afflictions fall upon us, such texts come back full of instruction and comfort. And prayer, *stated* prayer, in addition to special occasional prayer, is always, I believe, blessed.

I was interrupted last night, and have hastily concluded this (Monday) morning in my laboratory. Excuse therefore the scrawl.

Your sincere friend.

THE following letter to a friend, long an invalid, like George Wilson, possesses the greater interest now that both of them—after long suffering here, and work nobly and bravely done—have passed within the veil, and know the truth on all the subjects so often discussed by them. The differences in their views were only on minor points; in the great essentials of religion they were at one.

September 7th, 1851.

MY DEAR D.,—I have waited till we were fairly at home again before writing in reply to your last letter, which must on no account remain unanswered. We reached this on Friday night by steamer, after a very sickening passage, which made work impossible; but to-day I am well again, and on this quiet Sabbath evening, with my heart full of thank-

fulness to God for all the 'journeying mercies'—as
our good old Presbyterian forefathers would have
called them—which we have enjoyed, I may appro-
priately write to you.

I should be most unworthy of the confidence you
place in me, if I did not meet it in kind. The last
time I was with you, we unintentionally landed in
a doctrinal discussion, and this time, equally unintentionally, the same thing happened, and both dis-
cussions turned very much on the same question.

I cannot regret that the question was raised, or
rather, seeing that it was unexpectedly encountered,
I cannot feel sorry that it was, however briefly, discussed. We should have been false to our own
convictions had we concealed from each other our
beliefs on so solemn a subject ; yet we are at one,
I think, in feeling that oral discussion is not the
best medium for earnest argument ; and both of
us have overpassed the time of life when contro-
versy is welcome even as a gymnastic, and are too
quick of temper to be serene debaters.

I thank you very sincerely for writing, and none
the less that I can so sympathize with all you write,

that the faintest trace of dogmatism is, I trust, effaced by reading it.

The awful question, What is the final destiny of the 'wicked?' is one to which I never *dare* give an answer. I have no unhesitating conviction on the subject. I have the longing desire to believe in the final restitution of all spirits to perfect unity with God. I have no favourite theory to serve by believing the opposite. I cannot say that my own convictions which are deepest, demand eternal punishment to satisfy their cravings. Tennyson, in his *In Memoriam*, has, in various passages, expressed my feelings on this subject in a way I could not do, but in which I fully sympathize. The end of my reflections on this great question has been neither a yes nor a no, but a sigh, and the exclamation, 'Shall not the Judge of all the earth do right?' A grave old Secession minister (Dr. Lawson) uttered my feelings completely when he said, in reference to the heathen, 'If I meet them in heaven, I shall be delighted to see them, and if I do not, I am certain that there will be a good reason for their absence.'

Willingly would I go further, but I cannot, however I long to do it. I have lost very near relations, and very dear friends, and I have awoke in the middle of the night with such appalling visions of their possible condition, that the very remembrance of them whilst I write makes my heart palpitate anew. Wisely and sagaciously did the Romish Church engage to redeem souls from suffering. What would I not give or do, in the way of labour, or penance, or money-gift, or unceasing prayer, if I thought I could change the state of the dead? Ah! my dear friend, it is sad to think of the living; but the dead, the changeless dead, the hopeless dead, I can only fold my hands, and bow my head, and say, 'The Lord, he is God.'

I cannot find a doctrine of restoration in the Bible. I do not say there is not such there. I do not wish to dogmatize on the subject. I have not read the Scriptures, minutely searching for proof either for or against such a doctrine. I have read them as a present guide to holiness, devotedness, and duty; but I will not attempt to conceal that I have found an awful solemnity per-

vading every part of the Bible, and a dread array of
threatenings and punishments, such as project a fearful shadow into the world to come.   I dare not
counsel myself or another to trust to a redemption
unrealized in this life.   I know not how much is real,
how much metaphorical, in the descriptions of the
world of woe.   I cannot offer any opinion on the
certain significance of such words as 'eternal' or
'everlasting;' but I find no book of the Bible that
does not speak of God's wrath as well as God's
love.   I pause at such passages as 'Knowing therefore the terrors of the Lord, we persuade men ;' 'If
the righteous *scarcely* be saved, where shall the
wicked and ungodly appear ?' 'It is a fearful thing
to fall into the hands of the living God.'   And
although I long every day more and more to
realize that we should flee to God's love, not flee
from his wrath, yet I feel that I need chastisement
and punishment, and cannot be left to be swayed
by his love alone.   Nor can I think that the physical tortures referred to in the Bible as part of the
punishment of the wicked, signify nothing ; for a
resurrected body must be the avenue of pleasurable

or painful sensation ; and if there be *future punish-ment at all*, it does not seem possible that the body should not partake of it. I dare advise no one to die counting all these things visions. I know from the hell which my own heart has been, that sin can multiply itself, and be its own avenger ; and I am not sure that a spirit left to itself, to the agonies of its own shame and remorse, and hate and despair, would not suffer the more if its unsuffering body left the soul free to prey upon itself.

But the subject is too awful and too dark to be long dwelt on. Very humbly would I speak con-cerning it. It is the dark horizon which surrounds the hill top, on which in this life we are. Our duties to God whilst here are plain ; our state hereafter is not.

Christ's death was so mighty and precious a sacri-fice that, in itself, it had efficacy to save a universe. It made all men salvable; and if it shall please God to save all men for the sake of Christ, shall a poor sinner like me do aught else than join with a louder voice in the universal Hosanna ? But in the Bible I cannot find the doctrine ; and I believe it to be quite beyond human power to say yes or no on the matter. The question was asked our Saviour himself, ' Are there many that be saved?' and he would not answer it ; nor has it been left to any other to reply. The solemn words still remain : ' Strait is the gate, and narrow is the way that leadeth unto life, and few there be that find it ;' and they are very grave and even fearful words for me.

And now I will have done. I think you and I agree in seeking to love and serve God through Christ, and by his Holy Spirit ; and that we should condemn every one who, trusting to hope of final restoration, neglected present duty, and 'sinned that grace might abound ;' and we will both, I think, confess that the world to come is to us, and to all men, a dim and solemn mystery. And lastly, we will both bow our heads, and say that God is just, and will vindicate his justice to all ; and to him, with lowly abasement, we will leave the hidden things which in his own good time he will reveal.

· THE following letters were written to a young lady, Miss Mary Bell Stodart, during her last illness. She died 8th August 1847, aged fourteen years and seven months.

Edinburgh, 20th May 1847.

DEAR MARY,—It was very kind of you and Aunt Mary to sympathize with me in the loss of my dear sister, your namesake. She had a great regard for you, and thought much of you in your illness ; for she knew by long experience what it is to be on a sick-bed, and felt much for you who have been so soon called upon to have your patience tried. My sister is now in heaven, and has met by this time, I doubt not, and talked joyfully with, your beloved mother, and my esteemed friend, your uncle Andrew, who have gone before us to the other world. I remember well what a gentle, sweet person your mother was ; and I am sure that if the spirits of the just are permitted in heaven to know what is going on in this earth, my Mary and your mother will think much about us, and pray to God often for you and me.

When I am about to do a foolish or a wicked thing, I am often turned aside by the reflection that perhaps my sister in heaven is watching me all the while, and with sad reproachful eyes gazing on me, and beseeching me to forbear. I used to write to my sister every day while she was alive, and I was separated from her ; and now I try to live so that, with the help of God's grace, and through his aid, I may not offend my risen Redeemer, through whom alone I hope to join my dear sister. Yet, my dear Mary, the world of spirits is totally hidden from us, and we cannot tell how the happy inhabitants of heaven are occupied, though we are quite certain that they are with Christ, which is far better than being here. It may be that they are all ' asleep in Jesus,' so far as the earth is concerned, and are designedly spared the sadness of witnessing the sin and the suffering which are going on in this world of woe, and are debarred from knowing what their relatives on earth are doing, so that it would not be wise, Mary, for you or for me to trust to the prayers of our departed friends to bring down blessings upon us, or to count upon them as able to secure our reaching heaven. It was Christ that took our beloved ones to heaven; and it is he, and not they, as themselves would tell us, that can bring you and me thither. When it will please God to call any of us out of this world none of us know. How many persons will die before you and me has not been revealed to us. Whether we shall live to be old people, or be sent for very soon, is hidden from the eyes of all. Whether you or I shall first be summoned we cannot discover; but God sometimes shows his love to his children by not leaving them for a great number of years in this wicked world, exposed to sorrows, and trials, and temptations, and mercifully takes them to himself, 'from the evil to come.' It may please God to manifest this kindness to you or to me, and to give us very soon the great and unspeakable pleasure of beholding him, face to face, and joining our dear friends in heaven. And you have a better chance of that mercy than I have, for Christ has declared that he has a peculiar love for those that are young, and that 'of such is the kingdom of heaven.' So I think, Mary, you will perhaps get the start of me, for you are much younger (but we cannot be sure), and hear the Saviour say, 'Mary, rise, the Master calleth,' before death holds out his hand to me. At all events, we cannot reach heaven without dying, and we must be holy, even as Christ is holy, else we will not be admitted there. Now I am sure you will agree with me in thinking, that death is a solemn, almost a fearful thing to think of, and that, if it were possible, we should be glad to escape it altogether. But we cannot escape it; neither, if we could, would heaven open its gates for us unless we were holy beings. There are two things then, my dear friend, that you and I have to think about. The one is, how to meet death; the other, how to become holy. And as neither of us knows how soon the call may come for us to leave this world, and as both of us are not

stout, healthy, robust persons, but rather the opposite, we should be very greatly to blame if
we were to neglect to think of death and judgment as things awaiting us. Now, is it not a joyful
thought, my dear Mary, that Jesus Christ himself,
our beloved Lord and Master, is both able and
willing, not only to prepare us for dying, and to be
with us to comfort and support us in the hour and
moment of death; but is also equally ready and
desirous to open the gates of heaven for us, and
to impute to us, and clothe us over with, his own
holiness, without which we cannot be admitted
into the presence of the most holy God?

Such was the love of Christ to guilty man, that
though he was the Son of God, possessed of in-
conceivably great glory, and happiness, and holiness, yet he humbled himself so much that he
became a man, and endured all the trials, and
sorrows, and sufferings, and temptations that you
and I have undergone; although, unlike us, he
never thought a sinful thought or did a sinful
deed, but was 'holy, harmless, undefiled, and
separate from sinners.' And what is more, Mary,

although you have suffered much sore pain, and known many sorrows, as I have also, yet neither of us has undergone sufferings at all to be compared with those the Saviour suffered both in mind and body. We are reluctant and unwilling sufferers, but he willingly and joyfully resigned himself to suffer, and to die a cruel death to atone to God the Father, and to be the propitiation 'for the sins of the whole world.' Yet, my dear Mary, though he has assured us that he tasted of death for every man, and that he is able to save them to the uttermost that come unto God by him, we are also told in the New Testament, that he will not save us from the just wrath of God, or keep off punishment (eternal punishment) from us, unless we *do* come to him. And unless the Holy Spirit assist us, we can never acknowledge our sinfulness, or see how hateful a thing in the eyes of the most high and holy God is the breaking of his just and perfect law. But God is not more holy and just than he is merciful. He is long-suffering, full of compassion, slow to anger, and, as he has assured us, 'plenteous in mercy.' He has told us, 'If any of you lack wisdom, let him ask of God, that giveth to all men liberally, and upbraideth not; and it shall be given him.' Pray to God, then, dear Mary, and he will send you the Good Spirit to teach you to say, 'God be merciful to me, a sinner, for thy Son Christ Jesus' sake.' 'Lord, I believe, help thou mine unbelief.' Many of us will also pray for you. May God the Father, Son, and Holy Spirit bless you and redeem you from all evil!

May 30th, 1847.

DEAR MARY,—Now that you are back to the pleasant country, and the warm weather is making everything so beautiful, I trust it will not prove unwelcome to you, if I send you a few lines. You have been greatly in my thoughts since you left Edinburgh, and on this first Sabbath evening I have hoped you would not take it unkind if I exchanged with you a few Sabbath ideas concerning the great God and Father of us all, and his Son Jesus Christ, and the Holy Spirit, by whom we have access through Christ unto the Father.

Our blessed Redeemer is spoken of under many different figures or characters in the Bible, for, as it was impossible for us to understand or appreciate his exalted and divine nature, unless it were made familiar to us by what our limited faculties can comprehend, it has pleased God in his infinite kindness towards men to liken Christ Jesus to many objects quite familiar to us, so as thereby to prevent the possibility of our misapprehending his office, and feelings towards us. He is spoken of, for example, as a Plant, a 'plant of renown,' a Vine, a Branch, a Rock, a Lamb; and many other comparisons are used, all of them intended to supply us with instruction concerning Christ's relation to us and our relation to him. There is one of the characters under which Christ is referred to in the Bible so very beautiful that I should be glad, without fatiguing you, my dear Mary, to refer to it very shortly.

Our Saviour is called a shepherd — the great Shepherd of the sheep — and we are spoken of as his flock, his sheep, the objects of his thought and care. If you will look at the 10th chapter of John, you will find the account of an address, which I have no doubt you have often read, containing Christ's own statement to his disciples of his being the Shepherd, and a reference to who are his sheep, and who are not. There are three things alluded to in this beautiful parable which are full of instruction and comfort. In the first place, a sheepfold is referred to, a place of security into which the sheep can enter and be safe ; secondly, there is a wolf prowling round the fold, seeking to devour the sheep, and certain, sooner or later, to make a prey of all who enter not in by the appointed way ; thirdly, there is a good shepherd, who does not, like a hireling, flee when the wolf cometh after the sheep, but on the other hand, loves them so well that he lays down his life for his flock, and so saves their lives from the destroyer.

The meaning of this beautiful parable, my dear Mary, is not far to seek. From other portions of the Bible we have no difficulty in interpreting what it teaches. The sheepfold is the church of Christ, planted in the midst of a world lying in wickedness. That church consists of all those whom it has pleased God to call to be members of it, by showing them the sinfulness of sin, the wickedness of rebelling against a righteous and all-holy being, their Creator, Sustainer, and righteous Lord and Judge. The members of Christ's flock have also been visited by the Holy Spirit, who has renewed their natures, giving them a love of holiness instead of the love of sin, which is the original occupant of all our hearts; and they have received faith, which is the gift of God, so as to have confidence in Christ Jesus as their Saviour, whose blood cleanseth from all sin, and who has atoned to God the Father for all their great guilt.

There are many members of the church of Christ in those worshipping assemblies which men call the Church of Scotland, of England, the Free Church, and the like. But remember, my dear friend, that to be admitted into the visible church as members is not in itself a sufficient proof that we have entered into the fold of Christ. Those who admit us are men, pious, good men it may be, but not, like God, omniscient, so that they are liable to mistake. Unless we live an upright, holy life, preferring God's service to all other work, and know that we are building our hopes of salvation solely on Christ, the fact of our being members of a church will do us no good. The wolf who is mentioned in the parable, there can be no doubt, is Satan, who in another part of the New Testament is called a 'roaring lion, going about seeking whom he may devour.' These comparisons convey an appalling idea of the power of him who tempted our first parents, and still, though he be hidden from our sight, continues to tempt us all. We are poor, helpless, silly sheep. You, Mary, are a little, or at least (for they tell me you have grown tall) a young lamb. The enemy of our souls is a cunning, ferocious, cruel wild beast, able, if we fall into his hands, to inflict on us the greatest torments, and even eternal death. But to match this wily, subtle, fearful foe, there is the good Shepherd. Satan's power, though great, is limited ; but Christ is omnipotent. If we are members of Christ's flock, we are safe from the destroyer's hand. 'For this purpose the Son of God was manifested, that he might destroy the works of the devil' (1 John iv. 8). And he did destroy them, so that all his chosen ones are safe from the evil one. Our Saviour himself said, 'I give unto them (my sheep) eternal life'; and they shall never perish, neither shall any pluck them out of my hand' (John x. 28). And how was it that the Saviour overcame Satan? He laid down his life, he offered up himself to God, and ransomed the erring, straying sheep from the consequences of their own sinful departure from God, which was leading them into the jaws of the infernal wolf. Yes! my dear Mary, the great and good Shepherd, the Son of God, who was one with the Father, became himself like the flock he died to save. The wolf could not reach or touch him as the Shepherd; it knew his power, and feared and avoided him, whilst it hated him. But he became a lamb, even the 'Lamb of God, that taketh away the sin of the world;' like the flock, inasmuch as he was a lamb, but differing in this, that he alone was 'a lamb without blemish and without spot,' whereas they

were all crippled, blemished, and diseased. And
as a lamb he was the object of the wolf-like Satan's
fiercest cruelties. The prophet Isaiah tells how he
was treated (Isa. liii.) : ' He was wounded for our
transgressions, he was bruised for our iniquities :
the chastisement of our peace was upon him, and
with his stripes we are healed.' 'All we like sheep
have gone astray ; we have turned every one to
his own way, and the Lord hath laid on him the
iniquity of us all.' He suffered and he died, and
God in fulfilment of his promise, and in recompense of these sufferings, which he accepted as an
atonement for the slights and insults men had
shown him in rebelling against him, breaking his
laws and following the devices of Satan, he *pardoned* all, and pardons all who confess their guilt,
and plead the sufferings and the merits of Christ
as the ground of their acceptance with God. Dear
Mary, are you yet within the fold, or are you still
without, exposed to the devouring adversary ? He
will have as little mercy on a lamb as on a sheep
if you become his prey. Safety can only be had
in the fold, into which if any one enter, ' he shall

be saved, and go in and out, and find pasture '
(John x. 9).

DEAR MARY, — I am not about to write a
long letter, nor can I tell you anything which the
kind friends about you cannot tell you much
better. Moreover, in good books, and most of all
in the best of books, you will find written in the
most persuasive language, by the hands of inspired
men, what concerns all of us most to know. I
will, nevertheless, my dear Mary, trouble you with
this one letter more—though writing is much less
pleasant to read than print—as the last letter was
unfinished.

I remember so well when I was very ill, and
this more than once, and when the prospect of
restoration, even to indifferent health, was very
small, that I realized for the first time how little
our best and kindest friends can do for us in the
way of help, when we are in deep affliction and
death appears near. They can weep with us, feel
for us, pray for us, minister to our wants, and

strive to lessen our sufferings ; but beyond a certain point they cannot go. They cannot share our agony and relieve us of a portion of it, lessening its burden by bearing a part. They cannot impart their natures to us, or communicate to us the health of their bodies and the peace of their souls, in exchange for the disease and anguish of ours. They may go with us *to* the gates of death, but they are unable to keep us company *within* them. Alone, we must all enter the invisible world, so far as human comrades are concerned.

You have perhaps, Mary, patient and contented sufferer though you be, felt the force of thoughts like these. In the long and weary nights, when sleep would not come, and none was near to comfort you, you may have longed for help, and wished, many a time, that a friend were near. Such, at least, were my wishes, and great were my thanksgivings to God when he taught me to know that, 'like as a father pitieth his children, so the Lord pitieth them that fear him. For he knoweth our frame ; he remembereth that we are dust' (Ps. ciii. 13, 14). Both in the Old and New Testament, God's people are assured that they will not be deserted in their time of trouble, nor at the hour of death. They are told, on the other hand, that God sympathizes with his servants when they are afflicted, and they are promised his assistance and support. In the 63d chapter of Isaiah, for example, there is a very beautiful assurance to this effect, in reference to the ancient Jews : 'So he was their Saviour. In all their affliction he was afflicted, and the angel of his presence saved them : in his love and in his pity he redeemed them ; and he bare them, and carried them all the days of old ' (verses 8, 9). If you read the whole chapter, which is full of prophetical reference to our Saviour, you will see that it contains the same idea we were referring to in the last letter. The Lord is spoken of as a Shepherd, bearing and carrying those of his flock who were crippled and helpless, and could not walk alone.

What an idea it conveys of his love for men, that it should be said of him, that in all the afflictions of his people he was afflicted ! What an inducement to you and to me, to beseech God to make us his servants, that we may have a claim on his sympathy, and be able to count upon him bearing and carrying us when we are too weak to walk alone, and, but for higher than earthly help, must become the Satanic wolf's prey.

And then, Mary, for you there is the special consolation that for the youngest members of his flock Christ has a peculiar care. I am twice as old as you. I am one of the sheep; you, as a member of the chosen flock, will be one of the lambs. Here then is additional joy for you. In the 40th chapter of Isaiah we are told (verse 11th), in a passage prophetical of Christ, ' He shall feed his flock like a shepherd ; *he shall gather the lambs with his arm, and carry them in his bosom,* and shall gently lead those that are with young.' Our blessed Lord and Master does not show love merely to great and tried men, like his chosen servant, Dr. Chalmers, whom he has recently taken to himself, but he suffers little children to come unto him, and not only forbids them not, but declares that of such is the kingdom of heaven. He told his favoured apostle Peter, after his resurrection, and when he was about to ascend to heaven, to 'feed his lambs,' and he bears himself in heaven the title of ' the Lamb that was slain.'

If we had known only that Christ was God, we might have trembled to approach him in prayer, lest his holy infinite Spirit should be so far removed from communicating with our souls, that though he had pity for us, we could not count on him having fellow-feeling with us. But when we are assured that 'the great Shepherd of the sheep' is also 'the Lamb of God,' and possessed, while on earth, not only a divine nature which made him equal to God, so that he said, 'I and the Father are one,' but also a human nature equal to ours, yet sinless, so that he taught the apostle Paul to say of him, ' Both he that sanctifieth and they who are sanctified are all of one : for which cause he is not ashamed to call them brethren ' (Hebrews ii. 11). And again, ' Forasmuch then as the children are partakers of flesh and blood, he also himself likewise took part of the same,' verse 14th. When we know this, and that 'we have not an high priest which cannot be touched with the feeling of our infirmities ; but was in all points tempted like as we are, yet without sin' (Hebrews iv. 15), then we can come boldly unto the throne of grace, that we may obtain mercy, and find grace to help in time of need.

Ah then! dearest Mary, if you have not gone already, go now, humbly but boldly, to the throne of grace. Christ not only ever liveth, but liveth to make intercession for us. 'He tasted death for every man,' that is, for every child of man, and therefore for you. Till you plead his death as a ground for forgiveness, eternal life cannot be given by God the Father; but if you confess your sins, 'He is faithful and just to forgive us our sins, and to cleanse us from all unrighteousness' (1 John i. 9).

There is no mystery in the *way* of salvation, although many of its accessories are mysterious. Faith is the gift of God, but it is given to all who *perseveringly* ask for it. I close this letter with Christ's own assurance, 'Ask, and it shall be given you; seek, and ye *shall* find; knock, and it *shall* be opened unto you: for every one that asketh, receiveth; and he that seeketh, findeth; and to him that knocketh, it *shall* be opened' (Matthew vii. 7, 8).

July 4th, 1847.

DEAR MARY,—The long summer days have reached their longest, and are now beginning slowly to grow, little by little, shorter and shorter, and will dwindle by degrees through the pleasant autumn, till they are swallowed up by darkness and winter. And each of our days is like a summer day ; beginning with its feeble dawn of childhood, reaching more or less quickly its mid-day of greatest brightness, and fading down into grey twilight, and dying out into midnight darkness.

To some of us God gives lives like the days in June,—long and bright, warm and sunny, full of birds and flowers, leafy trees, blue skies, and all pleasant things. And the lives of others of us are December days, short and cold and chilly, with skies overcast, and snow upon the ground, the flowers dead, the trees bare, and no voice of the turtle-dove heard singing in the land. Yet after all, the difference in length between the longest and the shortest day of the year is not very great, and for every one of them there is the same ending—'the night cometh.'

Whether your life and mine are designed to be spring, or summer, or autumn, or winter days, is known only to him who is the 'Ancient of days.' God has shown both of us, I think, too many mercies to entitle us to speak sorrowfully of our lives, as if they were, so far as they have yet gone, deserving of the title of winter days. Yet he has laid his hand too heavily on us also, to make it consistent with truth, to affirm that they have been like days in June. On the whole, perhaps, they have most resembled

'The uncertain glory of an April day,
That now shows all the beauty of the sun,
And by and by a cloud takes all away.'

The morning of your life, dear Mary, has been overcast, as the spring mornings so often are, and ' the clouds have returned after the rain.' Yet what of that? 'as our day is, so shall our strength be.' That encouraging sentence, my patient, suffering, gentle friend, is worth a whole century of life to you and to me. God has told us that to cheer us; and, at the same time, has added, to warn us, 'Work while it is called to-day; the night cometh, when no man can work.' Long day or short day, there is the night at last; long life or short life, after so many beats of. the watch, it will be swallowed up in death.

God has promised, however, to those that love him, 'length of days.' The days in heaven are all June days. 'There is no night there.' And so, 'if we have tasted that the Lord is gracious,' we need not be very solicitous about the lengthening of our sojourn here. The shorter our earthly life, the longer our heavenly one; the less of time, the more of eternity; the sooner the frail garments of our sinful, perishing bodies are withdrawn from us, the more swiftly will the robe of Christ's imputed righteousness, and the vestments of immortality be put upon us. Wherefore, dear Mary, 'Let us comfort ourselves with these words.'

And then we come back to what we were speaking of last Sabbath: the willingness of God to listen to prayer, and his solemn promise to answer it. What we are to pray for is, the forgiveness of our

sins, and the purification, the sanctifying of our sinful natures. The mere forgiveness of our past sins
is not enough; for if our natures remain sinful, we
shall just begin sinning the moment after we are
pardoned. A river poisoned, by something added
to the water, might be purified; but that would do
very little good if the fountain or well from which
the river ran, had an inexhaustible amount of
poison in it. Our thoughts and actions are, as it
were, the drops and waves of a river poisoned by
sin; and our hearts or souls are the wells full of
sin, out of which our thoughts proceed. We have
to ask God accordingly, not only 'to blot out our
transgressions,' 'to forgive our evil thoughts,' but
also to render unsinful our evil natures. And this
poisoned well of our sinful hearts cannot, once for
all, in this world, be rendered pure and innocent.
Sin is like the poison in a serpent's fang, or a
wasp's sting, constantly renewing and reproducing
itself. You may remove the deadly juice from the
cup of a noxious flower; but if you go back next
day, the cup has gathered its poison again. Our
hearts are such cups. Day by day, hour by hour, '

moment by moment, they are seeking to re-fill themselves with what God hates. And only the Holy Spirit's unceasing influence is sufficient to empty them of sin, and fill them with holiness. In heaven the blessed Spirit shall so abundantly vouchsafe his power and grace, that sin shall be excluded utterly from the renewed nature of the redeemed. But on this earth there is a constant struggle in *all* Christian hearts between sin and holiness; and constant, earnest, prevailing prayer is necessary, that the Holy Spirit may be granted, not once, but continually, — first to renew, and then to maintain in a state of renewal, our otherwise evil natures. We are all by nature 'the children of wrath.' 'Our hearts are deceitful above all things, and desperately wicked.' That is true of you and me, amiable and gentle though you are, as it is of those whom men, even wicked men, abhor for their tremendous guilt. There are degrees of wickedness; and we have just reason for thankfulness that God has not allowed us to fall into the fearful sins others have committed. But the best of us have, nevertheless, in the eye of God, and in our own eyes, if sin did not blind them, a deceitful and desperately wicked heart. But God is 'greater than our hearts,' and Christ died for the 'chief of sinners,' and the Holy Spirit is given to them that ask for him. Ah! then, dear Mary, there is hope for you and for me that 'sin shall not have dominion over us.' You and I have earnestly prayed for the Spirit, and has not God answered us? Have you not *some* hatred of sin? *some* love of holiness? *some* perception of Christ's great compassion? If so, then it is of the Blessed Spirit's help; and you have learned that most important of all lessons, that God hears and answers prayers; not merely other people's prayers, but even yours. And what remains but to pray on, 'until the day dawn, and the day-star arise in your heart;' and to pray still, till God, who permits importunity, 'avenge thee of thine adversary,' the devil, and give thee assurance of salvation, and fill thy heart with 'the perfect love that casteth out fear.' For the present I close with a prayer, — 'The Lord bless thee, and keep thee; the Lord make his face shine upon thee, and be gracious unto thee; the

Lord lift up his countenance upon thee, and give thee peace' (Numbers vi. 24-26).

July 5th, 1847.

DEAR MARY,—I have been much pained to learn that you are still very poorly, though favoured by God with freedom from pain, and some of the other accompaniments of illness. ' Weary days and nights have been appointed to you ;' and I know from experience that it does not need sleeplessness, or loss of appetite, or severe anguish, to make them very weary. 'Ye have need of patience,' says the apostle,—a lesson we all require to learn and to practise, but which God in his providence is bringing home every moment to you. Faith and patience are two of the highest Christian virtues, and those who exhibit and exercise them ' inherit the promises.'

I hope your brother keeps better. God bless both of you, and hide you from evil, under his almighty wings.

July 10*th*, 1847.

DEAR MARY, — Day before yesterday I saw Miss Abernethy, who had received a letter from Aunt Mary, in which you were specially mentioned. I learned with renewed sorrow that illness still lay heavily upon you, and that you were confined nearly all day to bed. How much and how deeply I sympathize with you, I will not and cannot attempt to say. You are much in my thoughts, and daily remembered in my prayers. But whilst I found nothing but pain in the account of your bodily illness, there was something very solemn and cheering in the statement your aunt's letter contained that you were prepared for the worst. I rejoiced greatly, deeply, to learn that you were ready to abide by God's decision, and were contentedly and submissively waiting for the end. Ah! dearest Mary, to be able to do that, in the spirit of reliance on him who has sworn never to leave nor forsake those who put their trust in him, is to have attained to the kingdom of God. To be ready for the worst, is to be best fitted for

all the blessings being continued to us. The fear
of death is the greatest of all terrors. The love
of death, for its own sake, cannot be : God has
not asked *that* at our hands. He has made it
impossible for us to .put from us the love of life ;
all that he desires is, that we should prefer eternal
life to the few and fleeting years which make up
the sum of the longest pilgrimage here. There
may be as great discontent in wishing to die as
in wishing to live. To be conformed to God's
will, and be ready to live or equally ready to die,
is the spirit for which we should strive. When
Christ prayed for his disciples, shortly before he
was taken from them, his words were, ' I pray *not*
that thou shouldest take them out of the world,
but that thou shouldest keep them from the evil '
(John xvii. 15).

We have not two lessons to learn, one how to
live, the other how to die. One teaching imparts
the instruction needful for both. Holiness is the
thing essential to both. It is sin that makes so
many lives unhappy, and so many deathbeds full
of anguish. We are apt sometimes, I think, to

murmur at God's so solemnly insisting on holiness. Is he not all-powerful, and all-merciful? Might he not then forgive us simply as we are, cancel the charges against us, and, considering that we are weak and helpless creatures, excuse us being unholy, and take us to heaven as we are? We would not be very wicked; we think it quite proper that stealing, and lying, and murder should be severely punished; but might we not, at least, be allowed to indulge our own, as we call them, innocent thoughts, and in smaller matters have our own way? Yet if we think, what is this but as if a sick person should beseech his physician by no means to cure him completely, but on the other hand, should beg him, after restoring him to a certain point, to leave him there, with the seeds of the disease still in his system, ready at any time to grow up again into a poisonous tree which should kill him with its deadly emanations? No wise physician who had a patient intrusted to him would agree to such a request. He would say, 'I am a much better judge than you are what is best for you. Your wishes are tainted by the morbid state of your body. If I undertake your case at all, I must be allowed to eradicate every trace of disease from you. The treatment may not be always pleasant at the time; nay, will sometimes be as painful for me to inflict as for you to bear; but by and by you will be the first to thank me for not having spared you when you were sick, that thereby I might secure your perfect restoration to soundness of body.' And, in like manner, the great Physician of souls teaches us that he loves us too well to leave anything undone in the way of our moral cure. He will not be guilty of a kindness so mistaken as to relieve only the external symptoms of our spiritual distemper, and leave the deep roots untouched which may spring up afresh into the most frightful disorders. This earth is like a large nursery in which a great multitude of plants are sown. Certain of these the God and Father of our Lord Jesus Christ, who is 'the husbandman' (John xv. 1), intends ultimately to transplant to the banks of 'the river of the water of life' which proceeds out of the throne of God and of the Lamb, in heaven. All the seed which he sows grows up at first into stunted, withered, crooked, bitter, noxious weeds, because the enemy, who is the devil—and who likes much better to see tares and thorns and brambles growing than vines and corn—poisons all God's seed, and pours unwholesome waters on the roots, and blights them with killing frosts, and puts into each bud a worm to eat the heart of it, and hopes that that worm (which is sin) will never die, or the fire of its devouring be quenched. And the plants which turn away their leaves from the light which could heal them, and hang them down in the darkness, which they prefer (although God created them to love light and to hate darkness), would either perish, as many of them utterly do, or grow up into hateful things like the rank hemlock which the husbandman cuts down as cumbering the ground, and casts into the fire. But it pleases God to save chosen ones, not because there is anything more lovely and deserving of his care in some of these seeds than in others,—for none can claim his regards, or show a higher title than their neighbour's to his care. Guided by principles which he does not reveal to his creatures, but which are doubtless all just and wise, as everything that God does is, he selects certain of these seeds, and prepares them for becoming flowers that shall never fade, and branches that shall bring forth fruit unto life eternal. And think you, dearest Mary, that he will let so much as the shadow of evil rest upon the heaven-destined flowers, or allow one drop of the waters of sin to remain in the veins of the blossoms that are to expand in beauty in the holy place?

Many of the most beautiful plants in our gardens, and the trees that bear the richest fruits, were once way-side seeds, with insignificant flowers, or stunted thorny bushes, bearing only sour berries. It was a slow and troublesome process, however, requiring skill and pains and patience, that changed the buttercup into the ranunculus, or the sour crab into the sweet apple. And so, Mary, when it pleases God of his grace to select wild seeds, like you and me, we must not murmur or wonder if he insist upon wholly changing us, and leaving no portion of the original bitterness and harshness and sourness of our natural characters in us. Many of the seeds he chooses for himself, he allows just to germinate, and immediately plucks, and sanctifies, and takes to heaven. These are the babes who die in the very morning twilight of their days. Some, like the thief on the cross, have ripened almost to destruction, when they are snatched like 'brands from the burning.' Others, like Dr. Chalmers, are fostered long on this earth, and put on many of the heavenly characters before they are transplanted to the gardens of the Lord. But all are watered by the Holy Spirit, and redeemed by him in their whole natures, and purified and cleansed and pruned by the Father, the husbandman, and grafted into the true vine, which is Christ, and made branches of him, and thereby, and thereby alone, bring forth fruit.

Let us long then, dear Mary, for holiness. Even if we got into heaven without it, which is impossible, we should have no pleasure there. You and I know that sickness makes it impossible to enjoy the delights of this world, and that health is essential to the realization of even its pure joys. Well, sin is the sickness of heaven, and holiness its health. As a sick man turns away in disgust from the flowers and books and music and food that delight the healthy, so a sinner would find no plea-

Q

sure in the holiness of heaven.   Holiness and happiness are inseparable.   The Lord grant that, in his own good time, you and I, my beloved friend, may realize that great truth, and sit together at our Saviour's feet in heaven.

12th July 1847.

DEAR MARY,—I grieve to learn that you are still so poorly.   Nothing but a firm apprehension and remembrance of what God has told us, namely, that his thoughts are not as our thoughts, nor his ways as our ways, can reconcile us to perceive in his afflictive dispensations towards us, the hand of a loving Father.   We are all like the children who would rather die than take a bitter medicine, and think their parents and nurses very cruel when they compel them to swallow some unsavoury thing.   Yet the fondest of earthly fathers, even though his heart bleeds at sight of the unwise reluctance of his child, and at thought of the constraint he must use to induce him to take what is essential to his health, does not hesitate to make him drink the bitter draught, nay does it all the more the better he loves him.

And so we may be sure that our heavenly Father, who does not willingly afflict the children of men, has a purpose in all the sorrows he sends. The redeemed spirits in heaven probably are enabled to perceive the reasons why they were afflicted, and to rejoice that they underwent suffering.

Years even of pain and suffering, not to say days, will seem nothing, weighed against an eternity of glory, happiness, and immortality.

I do not write thus because I undervalue your sufferings. I recollect how little I used to esteem the counsels of those who exhorted me to patience when I was ill, but professed no sympathy with me. I hope you will not think that I despise or think lightly of your long and weary trial. Far otherwise. It is indeed the sincerity of my conviction that you have been so long very ill that makes me think of the need you have of the rich consolations of the God of all grace. That they are yours already I believe ; that they may be more and more amply vouchsafed, I pray.

25th July 1847.

DEAR MARY,—Allow me, in beginning another

letter, to express my deep and growing sympathy with you, my very dear friend, in your prolonged illness. I can so well realize from what I have witnessed, and what I have felt, how poorly you must be, that I grow sad at the thought of what you are suffering. Ah, how strange, how inexplicable, how intolerable, would our agonies be, to ourselves and to others, if we had not Christ to think of, as an example and a pattern of endurance, and the object of affliction ! The apostle Paul tells us that it became God 'to make the Captain of our salvation perfect through sufferings' (Hebrews ii. 10). The weary, sleepless nights you have to pass, the wasting, distressing cough, the fever, the thirst, the pain, are not in themselves joyous, but grievous. It is one of the blessed peculiarities of the Bible that it never makes light of our sorrows. I daresay you have met with some would-be consolers, who affect to persuade you that, after all, you have little to complain of. Even when they think otherwise themselves, they suppose it may do you some good to try to make you believe that you are well. The inspired writers never mock us in this way. They never refer to suffering as in itself desirable.

It is praised only when it leads those who bear it to know God as they did not know him before. It was not God that sent suffering into the world ; it was Satan and sin that brought it. But our Father who is in heaven brings good out of evil, and blesses, to those he loves, the afflictions he sends, as surely as the joys ; and accompanies sickness with marks of his favour not always granted to health.

And now that you are finding the earthly tabernacle of your wasting body dissolving, he is preparing a place for you, not made with hands, eternal in the heavens.

We are not like the heathens, with 'gods many, and lords many.' The Lord our God is one God. His oneness is revealed to us in a Trinity of Persons : these three are one ; and all are consenting to excite and to make worthy, and to render certain of an answer, every acceptable prayer. Jesus Christ is God, able to plead for us, and to satisfy God the Father's justice, by offering, in place of us, a sacrifice for sin ; by bearing for us the stripes we should have borne ; by paying for us the debt we in equity should, but never could have paid. And Christ is also Man, wearing in heaven a glorified humanity, and retaining a fellow-feeling with us in all our sufferings. We are taught to know that he suffered hunger, thirst, and pain, whilst on this earth; and are enjoined to believe that 'we have not an High Priest that cannot be touched with the feeling of our infirmities,' but one who sympathizes with his people, even in reference to our meanest bodily wants and commonest trials. He does not know our frame merely as the omniscient God who knows all things, or the omnipotent God who made our bodies and our souls, but likewise as the sinless fellow-man, who was tried and tempted in all points like as we are. It is a thought, dear Mary, to be kept fast hold of, as peculiarly consoling to one as you are, that Christ, as a sympathizing, affectionate 'Elder Brother,' is ever near to you, loving you with his own divine, unspeakable love; pointing you to himself as your Advocate with the Father; pouring forth his blood to cleanse you from sin; clothing you over with his imputed righteousness; and 'able to keep you from falling, and to present you faultless before the presence of his glory with exceeding joy.'

And there is this other precious thought, that the very inarticulate murmurs, the unworded groans, of God's people are listened to by him. The Holy Spirit grants his help most when his help is most needed. If there is promise of his blessed, indispensable presence when we are in the full energy of health, the promise is made double when we are brought low by sickness. Paul tells us, 'The Spirit also helpeth our infirmities,' etc. etc. 'The Spirit itself maketh intercession for us, with groanings which cannot be uttered' (Romans viii. 26). Our very murmurs and groans, if not the fruit of unchristian impatience, go up to God as prayers, and he has mercy upon us.

And the Father is 'faithful and just to forgive us our sins, and to cleanse us from all unrighteousness.' The whole Trinity are conspiring to keep all God's elect from falling or missing the end of their faith, the salvation of their souls.

I do not wish to fatigue you with a long letter; I will add, therefore, only a few words more. The beginning and ending of our hope of eternal life is Christ: keep, dearest, by him. We are very apt, in moments of depression, to forget this; to look in at ourselves, and, finding that we are full of sinful thoughts, and are altogether unprofitable servants, are prone to despair of his mercy, and then we ˙ try to make *ourselves* acceptable to him, and utterly fail.   If such thoughts disturb you, turn away at once from contemplating your own sinful doings; look outwards and upwards to Christ; plead his holiness, not your own.

Acknowledge your guilt, deplore your sin : ' God be merciful to me a sinner,' for Christ's sake, is the essence of Christian prayer.   ' Jesus Christ is the propitiation for our sins,' is the essence of believing faith.   ' Lord, I believe ; help thou mine unbelief,' should be the spirit of every petition. Keep, then, dearest Mary, by Christ.   ' For I am persuaded, that neither death nor life, nor angels nor principalities nor powers, nor things present nor things to come, nor height nor depth, nor any other creature, shall be able to separate us from the love of God, which is in Christ Jesus our Lord.'

EDINBURGH : T. CONSTABLE,

PRINTER TO THE QUEEN, AND TO THE UNIVERSITY.

www.ingramcontent.com/pod-product-compliance
Lightning Source LLC
Chambersburg PA
CBHW031358020726
47499CB00005B/1445